developer marketing

THE ESSENTIAL GUIDE

SLASHDATA

First Printing, September 2018

ISBN 9781717742223

VisionMobile Ltd trading as SlashData

19-21 Hatton Gardens

London, EC1N 8BA

United Kingdom

https://slashdata.co

CONTENTS

ABOUT THE AUTHORS

Authors are in alphabetical order by first name

Adam FitzGerald is responsible for Developer Marketing at Amazon Web Services. He oversees global technology evangelism, developer engagement programs, community building and startup marketing. His technical interests include fault-tolerant composable service architectures, infrastructure automation, and data science. Prior to joining Amazon, Adam ran Developer Relations for Pivotal, VMware, SpringSource, and BEA Systems. He is a recovering mathematician, aging gamer, occasional swimmer and proud geek parent.

Ana Schafer is director of Product Marketing for Qualcomm Technologies, Inc. where she oversees channel programs in support of the company's smartphone, compute, connectivity, and IoT businesses. Under her leadership the company introduced the Qualcomm® Advantage Network, a program designed to support business collaboration between Qualcomm and the companies selling, recommending and building solutions based on Qualcomm technologies. She is also responsible for the long-standing Qualcomm Developer Network, which has expanded over time to support not only mobile app developers targeting Qualcomm Snapdragon™ based smartphones, but also the burgeoning ecosystem of hardware and software engineers working in areas that range from XR, AI, robotics and IoT. Ana brings a breadth of experience to channel marketing at Qualcomm, having led developer-focused outreaches for over 10 years, and she was part of the pioneering effort with BREW that introduced one of the world's first app stores. She also led the marketing initiative for Qualcomm Technologies' reference design program for smartphones, working to provide ecosystem benefits across the device manufacturer, software provider and hardware component provider communities engaged with our reference designs.

Andreas Constantinou is Founder and CEO at SlashData. Andreas has been working at the crossroads of the mobile and software industries since 2000, helping take the very first smartphones to market. Since then he's worked with the top brand names in the software industry including Microsoft, Apple, Google, Facebook and Amazon. Over the past twelve years, Andreas has grown SlashData into the leading analyst firm in the developer economy, with a client base and reputation that out-rivals companies many times the size. In his academic life, Andreas is an Adjunct Professor at Lund University, Sweden, where he teaches Digital Business Models. He also founded the Athens chapter of EO Accelerator, the largest founder accelerator program globally. Andreas holds a Ph.D. from the University of Bristol, UK. Andreas has been diagnosed with acute self-improvement syndrome. He has a passion for book reading, training for triathlon and has a goal of visiting 48 new countries in the next 9 years!

Christine Jorgensen, Director of Product Marketing for Qualcomm Technologies, Inc., is helping to grow Qualcomm's developer community in areas such as Internet of Things (IoT), embedded computing, AI, and XR. As part of the Qualcomm Developer Network team, she creates compelling showcases of Qualcomm's compute and connectivity technologies to inspire next generation IoT and embedded solutions, and drive purchase intent of Qualcomm technologies. She also creates motivational projects which developers can leverage to accelerate their efforts from prototype to production devices. Christine has been with Qualcomm since 1997, in a variety of roles, including managing design and development of some of the first CDMA handsets, satellite phones, transportation and logistics products, and personal location tracking products and companion iOS and Android apps. Christine received a Bachelor of Science in Computer Science from University of California, Santa Barbara, and an MBA from University of San Diego.

Cliff Simpkins heads up Developer Audience Marketing for Microsoft Azure, helping bring the Microsoft cloud to life for developers around the world. He has been at Microsoft for the last 12 years, working in a variety of roles to help improve the lives of developers, including Developer Evangelism, Product Planning, Product Management, and Developer Marketing. His approach combines customer obsession with sound storytelling, working to land those stories with as little spin as possible. Prior to joining Microsoft, Cliff worked in governmental consulting and a couple of startups as a programmer.

Desiree Motamedi has almost two decades of experience building and executing successful go-to-market strategies. As Head of Developer Product Marketing at Facebook, she manages marketing to the developer ecosystem - through superior inbound, outbound, strategy and content. Her efforts are focused on getting developers excited about Facebook's global reach and innovation, with measurable results. She leads a growing team that drives the conversation around emerging technologies such as augmented reality, virtual reality, artificial intelligence, Building 8, and open source initiatives, on a global scale. Prior to joining Facebook, Desiree was Product Marketing Lead for Mobile Apps at Google. There she was responsible for rolling thunder marketing strategy for mobile app developers and built a vibrant developer ecosystem around the Mobile App Ads Platform, which includes AdMob, AdWords, and Google Analytics. She formed the cross-functional team comprised of various stakeholders touching mobile apps, and created a cohesive narrative for mobile apps across Google. A graduate of University of California, Santa Cruz, Desiree started her career in Silicon Valley with Adobe, where she spent over 7 years as Group Product Marketing Manager. She oversaw several product launches including the Adobe Flash Media Server family of products and repackaging of Creative Suite. Desiree's strength lies in her ability to orchestrate the efforts of multiple groups and coordinate with counterparts across teams from product marketing to PR to finance. She brings her technical knowledge, communication skills, and boundless energy into all her endeavors.

Jacob Lehrbaum is Vice President of Developer and Admin Relations at Salesforce where he helps developers and admins discover new career-paths and skill up via tools, videos and content on developer.salesforce.com and admin.salesforce.com. Jacob has held leadership roles in engineering, marketing, product marketing and developer relations over a 20-year career in the software industry, and is passionate about helping customers and developers transform their business and succeed with technology. Throughout his career, he has taken numerous products from vision to launch and has built and marketed disruptive open-source and cloud-based developer products at companies such as Sun Microsystems, Oracle, and Engine Yard.

Jo Stichbury is a freelance technical writer with 20 years' experience in the software industry, including 8 years of low-level mobile development. She is specialised in setting up new developer communities and populating them with useful content, having worked in this capacity at Nokia, Sony Ericsson, Symbian and Nature Publishing Group. Jo typically writes about software development, machine intelligence, computer games, electric and driverless vehicles, and the future of transport. She holds an MA and a PhD in Natural Sciences from the University of Cambridge.

Joe Silvagi is a Director of Customer Success for the HCI group at VMware and is VCDX #175. He has been in IT for over 20 years, roles ranging from administration, engineering, design, and management. Over the last 5 years at VMware he has worked in pre-sales along with various consulting roles. During his time with VMware he previously worked in the Hands-on Labs, helping to develop content and new ways of using technology, making building better content for the labs easier. He now works in Customer Success, leading a group of top architects to help ensure VMware's customers are successful with their products.

Katherine Miller currently leads the events program for the Google Cloud Developer Relations team. She has been at Google for nearly 13 years, and has worn many hats during her tenure - including scalable communications and marketing for agency products and programs, content strategy for large-scale developer events, and more recently, creating and leading global developer programs. She is driven by the desire to inform, educate, empower and drive success by bringing the right content to the right users. Prior to Google, she managed the pre-doctoral admissions process at Tufts University School of Dental Medicine - focusing on improving program diversity, served as a legislative fellow for the American Dental Education Association, and worked as a success coach for InsideTrack. She holds an MA from Stanford's Graduate School of Education (Policy, Organization and Leadership Studies), and graduated summa cum laude with BA in History from Hamilton College. Outside of work, Katherine runs for the all-women's Impala Racing Team, as well as after her husband Jason, 2 kids, and a cat.

Larry McDonough is the Director of Product Management for R&D Operations and Central Services at VMware. He oversees the VMware {code} Dev Portal and associated Developer Services, as well as the VMware Cloud Marketplace. Larry has spoken at conferences on his work in Developer Relations & Developer Evangelism, DevOps, Mobile App Development and Home Automation/IoT. Larry serves on the board of advisors for the University of California Riverside Bourns College of Engineering, and a few Silicon Valley startups including: Weavr, an innovative technology company focusing on new ways to engage developers and grow developer ecosystems. Previously, Larry led Developer Evangelism at BlackBerry, Java ME Product Management and JavaFX Engineering at Sun Microsystems, and managed the OpenGL APIs at Silicon Graphics. Larry has written code for NASA JPL, in the Pentagon for the US Department of Defense Joint Chiefs of Staff, at Walt Disney Studios, and was pictured in National Geographic Magazine demonstrating early full-body motion capture technology. Larry has a BSCS from UCR's Bourns College of Engineering and an MBA from UCLA's Anderson Graduate School of Management.

Luke Kilpatrick started as a Website Developer in 1996, transitioning to managing technology communities in 2007. In 2010 Luke moved to marketing program management as his full time role on VMware's social media marketing team. 2012 saw Luke at Sencha working in developer relations programs as well as focused social media, speaking at events around the world. In 2014, as Senior Developer Programs Manager, Luke managed Atlassian's ecosystem developer events and programs bringing hundreds of new apps to their marketplace. Recently he joined Nutanix as Senior Manager, Developer Marketing to bring an engaging experience to developers using their new PaaS products.

Matthew Pruitt is the Head of Global Community & Social Media at Unity Technologies, creator of the world's leading real-time 3D development platform. From indie developers to large enterprise development teams and gaming to architecture, the audience is diverse and the content distributed needs to speak to them all. He and his team oversee all social media marketing and community campaigns across the company. Prior to Unity Technologies, Matthew spent time in multiple marketing and product roles at IGN Entertainment, Machinima, Electronic Arts, and Quicken Loans.

Neil Mansilla is the Head of Developer Experience (DevX) at Atlassian. His team provides support for, and advocates on behalf of all developers in the ecosystem - from vendors building apps sold in the Atlassian Marketplace, to customer developers building private apps and integrations for their own use. The DevX team also supports Atlassian's developer events, from helping to organize content and tracks to providing onsite developer support. Neil's career has been primarily focused on developer ecosystems and platforms. Prior to joining Atlassian, Neil served as Head of Apps Ecosystem & Marketplace at Poynt,

Vice President of Developer Relations at Runscope, Director of Developer Platform and Partnerships at Intel Services (Mashery), and founded a few tech companies across several verticals, including search, e-commerce, and healthcare.

Nicolas Sauvage is Senior Director of Ecosystem and Corporate Development at TDK-InvenSense, responsible for all strategic ecosystem relationships, including Google and Qualcomm, and other HW/SW/System companies. Nicolas was previously part of NXP Software management team, responsible for worldwide sales, and later P&L and product management of the OEM Business Line. Nicolas is an alumnus of Institut supérieur d'électronique et du numérique, London Business School, INSEAD and Stanford. Nicolas believes life is full of special moments and is deeply passionate about products that enhance these special moments. He moved to the Bay Area in 2017 after 12 years living in Asia.

Pablo Fraile is Director of Developer Ecosystems, for the Client line of Business at Arm. In his role, he works with the mobile software developer community to increase the quality and performance levels of applications such as gaming, and drive the adoption of APIs and standards across new ones like machine learning and virtual reality. Before joining Arm, Pablo worked at Frontier Smart in Cambridge. There, he fulfilled a number of technical and commercial roles before heading the product management team, where he directed their solution strategy and built partnerships with global players in content distribution, web and semiconductor industries. Previous to Frontier, he was part of the video and graphics team at Imagination Technologies.

Siddhartha Agarwal is Group Vice President of Product Management and Strategy at Oracle, responsible for division strategy and revenue growth (organic and inorganic) for Oracle Cloud Platform (PaaS) and Oracle Fusion Middleware across all product lines globally, a more than $4.5B business. Siddhartha is also responsible for driving Oracle's global developer initiative to ensure developers are building next generation cloud applications using Oracle's Cloud Platform, and seeing it as a modern, open, easy, and intelligent platform.

Known as a hands-on technical business leader developing and driving company strategy with "start-up" mentality, Siddhartha brings effective leadership qualities and market development skills to Oracle's lines of business. To this, add a deep technical background and experience in cloud-native application development, mobile/chatbots, and integration, blockchain, and security. He has a proven track record in general business management, product management and strategy, and enterprise/cloud software sales experience. Before rejoining Oracle in 2014 (he had previously worked at Oracle from 1994 through 1999), Siddhartha served as Vice President of Worldwide Field Operations for Zend Technologies Inc. He has an MS in Computer Science/Economics from Stanford University, a Bachelor of Engineering from Caltech, and a BA in Computer Science from Grinnell College.

Stephen Donnelly is the Technology Lead for Accenture's Software & Platform Industry group and the global lead for Developer Ecosystem Services, based out of Accenture's San Francisco office. Within this role he provides the technology strategy and vision for the group and acts as the technical lead for a number of global development teams. Accenture's Software & Platforms Industry recognizes that, by the very precise nature of being 'born digital', leading companies have interrupted business for incumbent industries such as media, communications, and retail, enabling the meteoric rise of the most valuable companies on earth. Accenture defines a developer ecosystem as a system of interconnected elements that developers engage with to build products and services on top of platforms. Stephen considers developers to represent the heartbeat of digital innovation, making a thriving developer ecosystem critically important to the success of any platform or technology. Before moving to the Bay Area in early 2016, he spent a number of years leading digital delivery teams, building over-the-top platforms for several telecommunications companies in Europe and the Americas.

Thomas Grassl is Global Head of Developer and Community Relations at SAP. With over 388 thousand customers, the SAP Community and Developer ecosystem is a leading program in the enterprise space. As an experienced marketer and developer at heart, he works closely with developers, community members, companies and startups around the world helping them learn and apply new technology innovations to solve complex business problems.

WHY HAVE WE WRITTEN THIS BOOK?

During the Future Developer Summit in October 2017, we realised that developer marketing is still a very young and very fragmented industry, with pockets of best practices locked within the companies that master them. What was evident during the Summit was that we needed a medium to spread knowledge, currently held behind closed doors, to the broader audience of developer marketing practitioners based within thousands of platform companies around the world.

A question we often get at SlashData is, "Can you help us understand how Amazon, Google or Microsoft practice developer marketing" (replace names with your favorite tech brands) and it's exactly what this book aims to accomplish. In fact, it is written by the leading practitioners themselves.

The vision behind the book has been both simple and powerful; become the standard textbook that every new recruit into developer marketing reads to immerse themselves into this brave new world. A book whose influence may extend well beyond the field of developer marketing, given that developers are the most marketing-averse audience out there, it could become a toolset for B2B marketers in many more industries.

As the influence of developers continues to grow, we believe in a near future where most technology companies will need to get up to speed with developer marketing, and build departments of people that understand and value developers, in much the same way that IT departments have become standard in most companies today, but were a rarity 20 years ago.

We brainstormed the book concept at the 2017 Future Developer Summit event, and invited leading practitioners from the best companies in the field to contribute to this Essential Guide, resulting in what you are now reading: the first edition of a book that shares the best practices and diversity of experience across the companies involved.

We invite you to give us feedback, tell us more about your own insights, or even offer your company the opportunity to contribute to the next edition at https://sdata.me/dev-marketing-book.

If you enjoy the book, please share it and encourage your fellow marketers to read it. All profits are donated to a worthy cause, details of which can be found on the website for the book at https://sdata.me/dev-marketing-guide.

Andreas Constantinou, CEO of SlashData
Nicolas Sauvage, Sr. Director Ecosystem at TDK-InvenSense

September 2018

ACKNOWLEDGMENTS

The momentum for this book has been astonishing, and we'd like to thank everyone who has given us insight and inspiration throughout our journey.

We'd particularly like to thank our Technical Editor, Jo Stichbury, whose light touch upon each chapter has brought consistency throughout and made the book more just than the sum of its not inconsiderable parts. Jo enthusiastically joined the project as a technical editor, and soon found herself spending her early morning hours working with each author to iterate and improve the chapters. Her experience, and helpful, friendly and positive guidance to each author, alongside her edits, brought chapters from a dozen authors with very different writing styles and personalities, together into a meaningful whole.

We are very excited to be able to share a foreword from Adam FitzGerald, the head of worldwide developer marketing at Amazon Web Services.

This book would not have been possible without the generosity of all who contributed their experience and insight to it. We would like to extend our appreciation to the authors and their teams for sharing their wisdom:

Ana Schafer Muroff: Senior Marketing Manager, Ecosystems Relations, Qualcomm

Christine Jorgensen: Director, Product Management - Qualcomm

Cliff Simpkins: Director, Azure Dev Marketing - Microsoft

Desiree Motamedi: Head of Developer Product Marketing - Facebook

Jacob Lehrbaum: Vice President of Developer and Admin Relations - Salesforce

Joe Silvagi: Director of Customer Success for the HCI group - VMware

Katherine Miller: Developer Relations Program Manager - Google Cloud

Larry McDonough: Director of Product Management for R&D Operations and Central Services - VMware

Luke Kilpatrick: Senior Manager, Developer Marketing - Nutanix

Matthew Pruitt: Head of Global Community & Social Media - Unity Technologies

Neil Mansilla: Head of Developer Experience (DevX) - Atlassian

Pablo Fraile: Director of Developer Ecosystems, for the Client line of Business - Arm

Siddhartha Agarwal: Group Vice President of Product Management and Strategy - Oracle

Stephen Donnelly: Head of Technology - Accenture Webscale Services

Thomas Grassl: Global Head of Developer and Community Relations - SAP.

The team at SlashData who carried on behind the scenes while the book got more complex and urgent in the summer months of 2018: Christoforos Eleftheriadis, who tirelessly project-managed the book publishing operations, from author legal agreements to setting up the Amazon self-publishing process (no, it's not as easy as it sounds), making it all look so effortless. Moschoula Kramvousanou who stepped in enthusiastically during the summer months to follow up with authors and reinvigorate their commitment to the project. Steve Vranas who designed the book cover with an obsession with typography no less deserving than today's state of the art in developer-focused design. Eva Christopoulou and Miljana Mitic, who led the marketing strategy and web presence behind the book, which is unfolding as this book goes to print. Christina Voskoglou and Stijn Schuermans from the analyst team who supported the book and provided the latest data on developer influence metrics. And finally the proofreader, Claire Sceeny, whose dedication and attention to detail brought consistency to this text.

Finally, we'd like to acknowledge the thousands of developers that take part in our surveys every six months at SlashData. They help us take the pulse of the software trends, from mobile to machine learning and from edge computing to cloud, which are continually evolving and shaping the future of computing innovation. Working in this industry is a constant learning experience and we wouldn't have it any other way.

Andreas Constantinou adds:
I tend to dislike acknowledgements written by multiple authors, as they fail to show the real people and minds behind the book.

And so I would hate to see this acknowledgement missing its most important entry: Nicolas Sauvage. He was the single person without whom this book would have never been possible. Nicolas hatched the idea, devised the master plan for the book and saw it through to completion; he met every single author in person to share the passion, vision and establish commitment from the 15 thought leaders who are contributing to this book. This is an amazing accomplishment given the hectic schedules of everyone involved. Nicolas engineered his way out of challenges - whether it was authors dropping out or changing - through caring support, perseverance, ingenuity and perhaps a touch of stubbornness too! When I initiated this project on behalf of SlashData I hadn't the slightest notion of how complex a project it would turn out to be, including getting authors from commitment to delivery, getting legal sign-off from the top platform companies that employ the authors, to guiding and steering each author to help readers get the most out of each chapter. Thank you Nicolas: in you I found a new friend and collaborator who is a source of inspiration.

Nicolas Sauvage adds:
While I have said many times that the best part of writing this book is to raise the bar of a nascent industry in such an important discipline, the best part really has been to work with my dear friend Andreas on a project we both care so much about. We have co-written blogs in the past, but this was nothing compared to working on this book project, since Andreas imposed on us the tall order of creating THE Essential Guide of Developers Marketing. Strategy is in many ways a language few speak well, but not only is Andreas fluent in strategy, he masters its grammar and structure in a way that uncover logics and value creation models visible to very few. This Essential Guide brings countless insights because Andreas is intentional and laser-focused about making sure everything he and his team touches brings value and insights to the next level. I can't wait to work on the second edition with him!

Andreas Constantinou, CEO of SlashData
Nicolas Sauvage, Sr. Director Ecosystem at TDK-InvenSense
September 2018

FOREWORD

Adam FitzGerald: Head of Worldwide Developer Marketing - Amazon Web Services

In 2011, Marc Andreessen published an article in the Wall Street Journal that stated, *"...software is eating the world."* (source https://sdata.me/KwFKhx).

In that article he identified that more and more major businesses are being run on software and are offering online services to their customers and partners. I strongly believe that the trends he described in 2011 are even more evident today. You can see it in the most successful companies on the global stock exchanges, in the high demand for software developers in the job market, and in the way digital citizens are demanding more from the businesses and government organizations with whom they interact. Today, every company needs to have a software strategy or risk being outmaneuvered by more agile and adaptive competitors that deliver what the customer wants more quickly, and in the format that is easiest for them to use.

When it comes to software, the connoisseurs of technology are the developers that build and use it every day. They are the masters of the compiler, the command line, the frameworks, the test suites, the deployment pipelines and the production systems. As businesses have pushed for more nimble technical solutions, developers have created agile development practices that improve code quality, reduce project timelines, and iteratively produce new features. DevOps techniques and cloud based infrastructure have enabled those solutions to be deployed more quickly, more cheaply and at a scale that can respond to global demand. The developers and site reliability engineers are the ones on call 24/7, alerted to every system anomaly or traffic spike. When something does go wrong, they are the people called upon to rollback updates, squash bugs, and restore order.

With these critical responsibilities, developers are calling the shots when it comes to technical decision making. C-level executives can no longer make decisions about technology use at their company as a favor to an old college buddy or because of a nice round of golf with a sales person. Developers are selecting tools, platforms and infrastructure to get the best results for the systems they are building.

Building a tool, an API or a platform that developers love can delight your customers, disrupt your competitors and transform your business. So, if you are a business that wants to move quickly and wants to use software as a way to compete in your market, you have to understand and engage with developers.

How do you reach out to developers and convince them to use your product? This may sound like a classic marketing problem, but if you apply traditional consumer marketing techniques to this audience you will be destined to fail because developers abhor marketing. Developers are analytical, careful, loyal, data-driven and extremely busy. They have little patience for marketing hype, sales pitches or buzzword-filled promises of future capabilities. They have real, concrete problems to solve, right there in front of them, and they want help from people and sources that they trust.

Fortunately, the experts who have written this book have spent decades of their careers thinking about how to engage with these developers. Their combined wisdom provides a map for you and your company to create the kinds of things that developers care about. Chapters in this book will describe how you can grow your developer community and how running a developer program for experts in the field will encourage them to advocate for you. You will learn about the dynamics within a developer community and also learn what you can control and what you cannot. This book also provides information about where you can find developers, both online and in real life, and how to hold a real conversation with them from organizing events to managing your online community. And, if you are not yet sure who you are conversing with, there is even a chapter on the use of developer personas. This book provides some extraordinary insights from those who have worked in the developer marketing field as it comes of age.

For me, developers are the fulcrum for business innovation. Over the coming decades, some companies will embrace developers, earn their trust and help them solve their technical problems. Those companies will be the most successful businesses of the 21st century.

Introduction | Developers Are a Big Deal. Marketing To Them Shouldn't Be

Jo Stichbury: Technical Editor - SlashData

Today, Peter Levine is an influential venture capitalist; his opinions are closely listened to and he controls large sums of money. In the 1980's and 1990's, Levine worked as a software engineer. He describes the extent of his influence on tool purchasing decisions at the time as follows:

"When I was a developer, I had no budget and I couldn't buy a pencil, when pencils were popular. I couldn't buy anything. Whatever central IT had ordered, that's what showed up on my desk."

Times have changed and developers are making implicit purchasing decisions having become powerful influencers in their own right. Understanding how to engage with developers is crucial for any company shipping any kind of software. Those companies selling platforms and tools need direct adoption of their products, while those offering apps and services want to extend their reach by ensuring compatibility and a common vision within their particular domain.

Engaging at C-level is no longer sufficient: the software developer is now a powerful force in decision-making. This book, from leading developer marketing practitioners working for some of today's largest platform companies, will teach you how to engage with developers to build a relationship that is both informative and empowering.

The power of developers

In working on this book, we have found a common theme running through its chapters: the nature of development has been permanently changed by the uptake of open source and the advent of cloud computing. Software developers today can readily find code and tools to evaluate, use and learn, and they are increasingly influential in their company's technology selection procedures.

The availability of open source code, and free-to-trial SDKs, has allowed developers to evaluate platforms and tools and choose what to use without having to ask their manager or procurement team to sign off on a license for paid software. They are increasingly in control over the process by which software enters their organisation, and as complexity increases, the managers to which they once deferred are now asking them to steer technology adoption decisions.

Similarly, developers can now easily adopt a cloud platform during the early phases of development and testing. They can instantly license, provision, and use tools that previously would have required evaluation and sign-off from their manager, a purchasing department or a system administrator sitting within IT. Delays and paperwork are avoided, and these developers can experiment and innovate, jumping head first into free trials, supported by dynamic communities that share goodwill in the form of code examples, instructional videos and expert discussion forums. Providing developers with the technical tools they need to be productive as they evaluate and protype is key, along with the means to scale up to production further down the line.

We can turn to data from our most recent SlashData Developer Economics survey, Q2 2018, to see if it confirms the anecdotal evidence about developer influence on purchasing. Insights from the survey are based on the responses of over 20,000 developers from across more than 150 countries. Our data shows that 68% of front-line developers were involved in software tooling decisions. Between 40% and 60% of developers said they were in a position to make recommendations or influence decisions. Separately, the survey found that more than a third of developers (including 38% of front-line developers) acquired tools for their personal use. This means they have at least some decision making power and at least a small budget to spend, but the key is that they act as a 'wedge point'. They can introduce tools and demonstrate their value to others based on actual experience and results, acting as evangelists across the organisation.

Our data also confirms that about a third of mid-level developer leaders (team leaders, architects, and product managers) are involved in specifying the tools used (35%, 32%, and 29%, respectively), or even get the final word on which tool to adopt (34%, 30%, and 33%). Although this shows that a majority of cases still need management to sign off on purchases, this is more likely to affect the pricing and positioning of tools, rather than which tools are selected (out of a set of competitors).

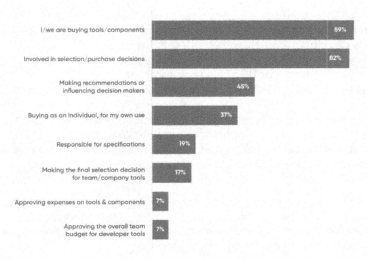

Developers are powerful influencers
% of professional developers (Q2 2018, n=13,917)

I/we are buying tools/components	89%
Involved in selection/purchase decisions	82%
Making recommendations or influencing decision makers	45%
Buying as an individual, for my own use	37%
Responsible for specifications	19%
Making the final selection decision for team/company tools	17%
Approving expenses on tools & components	7%
Approving the overall team budget for developer tools	7%

The days are over when an inadequate tool could be pushed from the top down. Decisions are increasingly made at lower organisational levels because of the complexity and fast-changing nature of software, combined with the myriad of back-end corporate systems with which to integrate.

So what *is* developer marketing?

It is worthwhile taking some time to differentiate the terms 'developer relations' and 'developer marketing', which are sometimes used interchangeably, but have different objectives.

If you, or your team - if you have one- work in *developer relations*, your responsibility is to build credibility, trust and influence. You will find yourself evangelising for your company by representing it at events, blogging and on social media, typically taking the role of a community manager. You will likely have the technical chops to write sample code and run demos. Developer relations is also about advocating for the external developers you encounter, representing them by giving their feedback to your technical teams to influence their product roadmap and strategy, and inputting defect reports and feature requests. Your role is a balance between representing the needs of external developers and evangelising your company's product.

If you or your team work in *developer marketing*, your role is to encourage third-party developers to learn about, try, adopt, use and even contribute to a software product. To be credible in front of a developer audience, you need to be able to communicate about your product at a detailed level without unnecessary marketing jargon or BS. This probably means having a technical background or at least sufficient experience in your domain to ensure you are taken seriously. Activities you would expect to be engaged in include creating the developer marketing strategy, segmentation of developers into personas, organising social media, content marketing and email campaigns, planning events and conferences, and steering developer rewards programs, developer advocacy programs and innovator funding/incubator programs.

Phew! That's a lot of ground, but, fear not. These topics, and more, are covered within this book, which focuses on developer marketing, rather than developer relations.

Finally, for completeness, let's define *developer product engineering*. In this team, you will build and deliver an SDK or

API to third party developers. You will be responsible for the strategy, roadmap and development of the tools and code needed in the SDK, and the technical content surrounding it, such as sample code and technical documentation. In the developer product engineering team, you will need the skills to provide answers in technical forums, write blog posts, and create content for webinars, video tutorials and training courses. And, if you are in developer marketing or developer relations, members of this team will be your go-to folks.

Having defined the terminology and clarified where this book will focus, we move on to one of the characteristics of the broad group we know as 'developers': their general dislike for marketing!

Raise your hand if you like marketing

It is a truism that developers hate marketing, because, well, who does like marketing? While some groups of people may find it more acceptable, particularly if it is well-executed, it is rare to find anyone who is keen to be the target of a marketing pitch! Perhaps a more insightful statement is that developers are particularly averse to generic, aggressive or repetitive messaging about tools, products and services. Instead, they want relevant and meaningful information and the opportunity to make up their own minds.

What you will take from this book is an understanding that the way to developers' hearts and minds is a two-way conversation. You need to show that you are sharing authentic information with them and that you are genuine about wanting feedback, so you can refine your product.

Developers particularly value the opinions of others like them, and want technology that is supported by a community of other developers like them; they want a community that is growing and is enthusiastic. They want to know that, when things go wrong, there's a place to ask a question and get a swift response 24/7, and to find that the answers to common issues are already there and easy to find, because the community is well-established.

As developer marketers, our role is to enable developers to make informed decisions, by giving them an opportunity to try our service out for themselves and join the community of those who use it. Many of the chapters in this book echo this sentiment and all describe how the authors and their companies understand this particular audience and engage with them.

Why should you read this book?

While countless books, courses and blogs exist for other forms of consumer and B2B marketing, developer marketing has been poorly served to date. This book is intended to be the 'textbook' for those working in marketing toward developers. If you are entering this domain, or already working in it and wanting to advance your career, it is for you too. We have intentionally kept each chapter short, and distilled the key insights of each contributing expert. It isn't a step-by-step guide to writing a developer marketing strategy, but instead a toolbox for you to gain the knowledge and practical understanding needed to work with your audience.

You will find this book useful if you're working in developer marketing in a technology company and want to learn how to build your ecosystem to attract, support, and grow your developer base. It isn't necessary to have experience, and perhaps you are just starting out on your developer marketing career, maybe transitioning from traditional marketing, or from working as a developer yourself. Whatever your experience, you know, or soon will know, that the developer audience is a tough one to market to. This book is designed to share best practice from thought leaders in this field. If you take away the insights of our contributors, you will be well on the way to handling any B2B marketing role!

Learn from the experts

In each chapter, our authors have been encouraged to share valuable but non-obvious learnings, including mistakes they've made along the way, and a set of actionable best practices.

We typically begin each chapter with a problem statement, to introduce the topic of the chapter and make clear why this topic is important to consider. Then we describe the company's 'journey', with a goal to share what does and does not work - and why, so you gain practical insight from the voice of experience.

We start the book with a fascinating chapter. Cliff Simpkins describes the value of using developer personas and how to define them. Cliff has spent a number of years at Microsoft building the developer personas used by various Windows groups, and he describes how they can make a difference in the product development and developer marketing lifecycle. If you're wondering about the difference between market segments and developer personas, well, both approaches break a larger market into smaller groups using shared characteristics (needs, interests, and habits). After all, there are many ways that you can divide and group an audience. However, the two approaches and outputs are quite different. Market segmentation tends to be a quantitative, or data-driven, process using exhibited/measurable behaviors or traits. It can be powerful when executing a marketing strategy and measuring its success. Developer personas are qualitative; they are defined by internal personal drivers and motivations, they are powerful for product and campaign creation. Cliff describes the best practices he has learned to enable you to develop personas that take root in your business.

The first mass marketing email was sent in 1978. Some forty years later, email marketing is still a key part of the developer marketing toolbox although times have changed in the way that email is read: these days, more emails are opened on mobile devices than on desktop computers. Facebook have a huge developer ecosystem to connect with, and in her chapter, Desiree Motamedi shares the best practices that her team use, with a deep dive into the email flow and some key insights into AB testing and data collection. To close the chapter Desiree discusses her vision for the future of Facebook email marketing to developers.

Our next chapter, from Jacob Lehrbaum, describes the power of community, and contains valuable insights about one of the most interesting and exciting areas of developer marketing: bringing people together. Jacob covers a number of the ways that developers working with Salesforce support and inspire one another, both online and in real life. Local developer groups are core to the Salesforce developer community, and have been carefully nurtured by the company, as the chapter describes. Many communities truly are greater than the sum of their parts, and understanding how to guide individuals and groups without interfering in the organic growth of the overall community is a great skill. The best practices in this chapter will set you up to understand developer community culture, pave the way for the community to grow, identify and inspire developer champions and teach you how to measure your success.

In a candid chapter, we learn how Oracle's traditional marketing was reinvented to meet the demands of the a new developer audience as Oracle introduced its cloud product. The early part of the chapter shares lessons learned about online developer engagement and Oracle's continuous education program. It is followed by some insights about the Oracle Code developer events, which have a huge reach across the web through streaming and on-demand video. Siddhartha Agarwal explains how to ensure balance in the programme of each event, and how to keep the tone relaxed and casual (he even includes some sartorial advice!). A great insight from this chapter is that, by running a number of events in rapid succession, it was possible to introduce rapid changes and learn iteratively, to get the best out every following meeting.

In the chapter provided by Thomas Grassl, who speaks of his experience at SAP, we learn how to find and engage with potential product evangelists. Nothing - or rather, nobody - speaks to developers better than one of their own. You will often find the best way to get your message across is through evangelism from existing customers. Developers will trust their peers, so you will find that it pays off to make heroes of your existing developer base and encourage them to advocate for you. Thomas explains how to do that, and the lessons that SAP have learned along the way.

In a chapter from Larry McDonough, we learn the background behind VMWare's Hands-on Labs, which came out of the necessity to be able to bring up a trial of VMware's product stack rapidly so it can be understood and explored by potential customers. To encourage developer uptake, VMWare needed to make their complex and extensive technology platform accessible and easy to learn, and they introduced Hands-on Labs for this purpose. However, the Hands-on Labs have expanded and brought additional and unexpected value to the company through beta and early access programs, certification and education.

A dive down under follows, with a chapter that gives us the inside story of the evolution of Atlassian's App Week. A key insight is that hackathons can be great to raise awareness of your product, but they often do not create lasting value. Atlassian ensure that at App Week, there is no competitive element, instead participants help each other, which encourages a level of trust in the community. Cooperation between vendors is worth more than any prize available from an event. For Atlassian, App Week encourages professionals to work together so they can collaborate to give combined, validated feedback, which proves invaluable to Atlassian's product managers, allowing them to focus attention on the areas of the platform that truly matter to developers. This insight is one of many about the nature of trust, and how to bring developers together in the real world.

In a stand-out chapter from Pablo Fraile, we find out about connecting with your developers and finding a way to their hearts and minds, even when they aren't easily captured. Arm have had this very challenge to overcome because of their relatively small size and lack of visibility (they don't make a physical product that developers directly interact with). Arm have wisely invested time and resources into identifying the needs of developers and their pain points. As the chapter describes, normal surveys and focus groups are good ways to get feedback from developers, but often a simple conversation at a conference can throw up a lot of useful feedback. It seems that, like everyone, developers love talking about what they don't like, and if you go away and do something about it, you can earn their trust, respect and loyalty. The authors also explain that the diversity of products using Arm means that they cannot hire and retain experts in every field, so they have introduced an Innovator Program to locate the people who have the most credibility within each of the target developer segments, and encourage them to accelerate and tell their story - and Arm's, alongside it.

The following chapter is titled "Hardware is the New Software", and the authors explain how Qualcomm set out to build a developer community around the DragonBoard™ 410c, which was designed for developers taking their first steps into IoT to quickly prototype new designs. The challenge was to encourage an existing community of mobile app developers to work with the new hardware, while also attracting an even larger community of hardware developers who were new to Qualcomm. The chapter shares some important insights about developer marketing to a very broad community. A key was prioritizing educational content to make building with hardware as easy as programming software.

In her chapter, Katherine Miller shares the best practices she has learned at Google on her journey to gain strategic value from developer events. The chapter is a behind-the-scenes view of how to plan and execute developer events. You'll learn how to optimize your return on investment - not only in the eyes of the finance team of your company - but also in the eyes of the developer audience. Events can tell stories by building brand awareness and positive sentiment, and also drive momentum around other impactful developer tools and programs. The goal is to provide technical sessions that leave the average audience attendee understanding approximately 2/3 of the content. You want them to leave engaged, having spotted an opportunity and inspired to head home and dig into something challenging and unfamiliar.

Matthew Pruitt explains how to get your entire organisation behind the effort of content marketing to developers, based on his experiences at Unity. In the chapter, he explains that the right mindset to frame your content marketing is "What is the one takeaway I want someone to have after viewing my content?" And "Why should they care?". It is essential to look at your project objectively and then for your content to reflect that objectivity. You don't want a potential user to make assumptions about your project, but since they don't know what you know because they didn't work on the project, you need a clearly communicated message. Your content should paint the full picture of what your product is, so the customer wants more: to try out the product, whatever it may be. Matthew talks through some of the most popular channels for content marketing, and gives a compelling case for making short-form videos and releasing them to YouTube.

Our closing chapter is an interview with Stephen Donnelly from Accenture that discusses the key themes we observed in putting this book together and his insights upon them. The chapter rounds off the book by touching on the discussion points of the preceding chapters, and it introduces some new areas to consider, such as how and where to present your technical content, like documentation, and who to ask to write it.

How you can help us

If you read this book, you can help by giving us feedback. What are you experiences as a developer, or as a developer marketing professional? What have we got right? What have we omitted? What is questionable? Please tell us! If we got it right, and you appreciate our efforts, please leave us a review on the book's website https://sdata.me/book-feedback. You can also use the link to volunteer to write a chapter for us in a future edition.

You are also helping a good cause if you bought this book. All profits are donated to a worthy cause. You can find out more on the website for this book at https://sdata.me/dev-marketing-guide.

Chapter 1 | Using Developer Personas To Stay Customer-Obsessed

Cliff Simpkins: Director, Azure Developer Marketing - Microsoft Corporation

Introduction

At Microsoft, our mission is to empower every person and every organization on the planet to achieve more. Since our founding moment, our customers have always been at the core of the platforms we build, making them more productive - from Altair BASIC to Windows, from Visual Studio to Office, from Minecraft to Azure.

But as your customer base scales, particularly when you build a platform, it becomes easy to lose or splinter your team's focus. As your scale grows, your engineers may start to build for who they know (themselves, their team, or the last three customers they spoke to last month); your product managers start to lean on analysts to tell them what to build; and your marketers can start to test their messaging with the developer team building the campaign website (yes, that happens!).

To keep your team aligned, you need to define what you want to achieve, and what success looks like. Most engineering teams today use product specs to keep folks aligned on the features and capabilities that they are building, but I posit that many companies today fail to clearly define why the product is being built in the first place,

My favorite tool for keeping everyone on the same page is the persona. About a decade ago, I started using user personas built by our usability labs team in engineering, but I've increasingly spent the last six years in product management building several evolutions of developer personas for use across Windows, covering mobile app developers to PC and console game studio developers, and helping mentor other teams on how to build developer personas as well.

In this chapter, I'll introduce personas within the context of a developer-centric company (as opposed to something P&G would take to market), and discuss how personas can make a difference in the product development and developer marketing lifecycle, highlighting a number of learnings I've had along the way.

As a little about me, I've been at Microsoft for over 12 years, in roles spanning developer evangelism, .NET product planning, product management for Windows Phone and Windows, and the last three years doing developer audience marketing. As I mentioned above, personas have increasingly been a core ingredient in my work over the last ten, first appearing when I was working on Windows Communication Foundation (WCF), and increasingly becoming more and more core to my work, and my team's work, with each passing year. In my final years at Windows, our three-question persona gearbox was core to everything we did - our research, our event registrations, and our developer program. We used them to build our content, plan our marketing campaigns, and how we did (by target persona). Hopefully by the end of this chapter, you should walk away with an understanding of what a good persona looks like, and a spark of interest in helping your team become more customer-obsessed.

Why developer personas matter

As products are built and brought to market, they should also carry a means of measuring success, whether it's an API, a user interface, a website, or a paid advertising campaign. But often, this measure of success isn't shared, and a team is neither clear nor consistent on what success looks like, leaving each team member with their own perspective on who will use their offering, and how they should use it. And, as a result, the product experience feels fragmented and mis-aligned. To bring everyone into alignment, the team needs a shared definition of where they are going and how they know when they have been successful.

For me, the need for this shared definition - a need for organizational alignment - happened around 2011 as my team discussed the keynote we were building for a major developer conference. In the room were executives from the different groups involved in the event - engineering, marketing, evangelism, and PR. As we discussed the keynote structure and flow, opinions and interests both meshed and clashed (as they often do). Each person spoke from a position of authority about audience needs, with the same refrain - '…but developers want…'. To support their point, each person flagged different, and sometimes conflicting, core audience needs, and the key aspects that they felt should be highlighted in flow and demos of the talk (e.g. business value, tooling advances, cool tech advances, productivity, etc.).

After the discussion, my PR guy and I talked about how fragmented our target 'developer' was for the event, and we started thinking about how we needed a common vision to anchor our narrative. We decided that the group needed some sort of shorthand that would allow us to break up the generic 'developer' into smaller, more defined communities that had defined pain points and aspirations. This, we reasoned, would allow us to discuss the keynote's scope (i.e., it's not for 'Peter', but instead for 'Paul' and 'Mary') and elevate the narrative beyond a feature-palooza.

In the year that followed, my team went on a journey to build out five developer personas, with a business focus on three of them: 'Ravi', 'Jerry', and 'Tyler'. Within two years, our developer personas became core team assets and a variable in our business planning - we structured our offers and programs based on the business and life goals of each persona, we included them in our marketing agency briefs, and we even based our competitive analysis on the personas. For example, we asked "how does an experienced independent developer ('Jerry') approach DevOps?" and compared the answer with a different persona, such as a line developer in a larger company ('Lana').

The magic of personas is that they provide a composite view of a larger audience, and they allow you to make that audience a part of your product's narrative. And while lots of industries use personas in their marketing, I personally believe they are crucial in developer marketing for one simple reason - developer personas provide an easy way for non-developers to understand this audience. Consumer and B2B marketing are both established disciplines, with defined approaches, best practices, and benchmarks. But developers behave differently: they evaluate and trial products differently, they value and consume content differently, and they prefer a different sales model.

Once we started using personas in our efforts, we found PR and developer marketing to be much easier and more effective.

What is a developer persona?

Wikipedia describes a persona as "a fictional character created to represent a user type that might use a site, brand, or product in a similar way....a representation of the goals and behavior of a hypothesized group of users. In most cases, personas are synthesized from data collected from interviews with users...They are captured in 1–2-page descriptions that include behavior patterns, goals, skills, attitudes, and the environment, with a few fictional personal details to make the persona a realistic character" (https://sdata.me/TodxCy).

As a simple example of a persona, I like to reference what I think of as developer persona canon, developed by Microsoft while working on Visual Studio 2005. In a 2004 blog post, Nikhil Kothari framed the essence of their three product personas:

- 'Mort', the opportunistic developer, likes to create quick-working solutions for immediate problems and focuses on productivity and learn as needed.

- 'Elvis', the pragmatic programmer, likes to create long-lasting solutions addressing the problem domain, and learn while working on the solution.

- 'Einstein', the paranoid programmer, likes to create the most efficient solution to a given problem, and typically learn in advance before working on the solution.

Back in 2004, these personas helped cleanly define what would be done for the VB programmer, the C# developer, and the C++

developer. Today, although technologies have evolved, I believe the core developer personas still exist - they just tend to use newer frameworks and models (e.g. Ruby, PHP, Go, TypeScript, etc.).

There is much more to these 2004 personas than the super simplistic statements, but they paint a crisp picture, They have even sparked much debate over the years within the developer community, with developers often complaining about the stereotyping and pigeon-holing that they can lead to, particularly for those falling into the 'Mort' label (an early incarnation of the modern malign of the 'script kiddy' by an 'elite programmer' of today).

To further clarify what a persona is, let's take a moment to also briefly examine a few other common practices that are used to describe a product's users, such as market segments and taxonomy attributes, and explore how a persona is different from each of these other approaches. It's important to note that what you use is not a binary choice - there are many folks (my group included) that use personas along with one or more of the approaches below.

Personas vs market segments

Wikipedia defines market segmentation as "the process of dividing a broad consumer or business market, normally consisting of existing and potential customers, into sub-groups of consumers (known as segments) based on some type of shared characteristics" (https://sdata.me/lCfoSw).

The use of market segments is most handy on the business-oriented side of the house because they're easy to build marketing programs upon. You can cleanly size an opportunity, you can build a lookalike audience pretty simply, and you can measure the ROI of your campaigns using easily observable audience attributes.

The idea of a market segment is similar to a persona; in fact, there are a number of folks that tend to use the two terms interchangeably. Both approaches break a larger market into smaller groups using shared characteristics (needs, interests, and habits). However, the two approaches and outputs are quite different. Market segmentation tends to be a quantitative, or data-driven, process using exhibited/measurable behaviors or

17

traits. User personas tend to be a qualitative process, using internal personal drivers and motivations.

As a marketing segment example, a marketing team might look at the same population of developers used for personas, and create the following market segments, starting from easily measured attributes such as where they work:

- 'Enterprise developers' work for large corporations with 1k+ employees, with a focus on building internal applications and services; they are productivity-minded and trend towards proprietary technology stacks.

- 'Emerging developers' work at startups and tend to be younger; they are very tech-forward and prefer building upon open stacks.

- 'Partner developers' work at platform or service companies, building offerings that increase the productivity of their customers.

The team might even further divide the market segments by their purchasing patterns, or perhaps further slicing by organization (community, academic, small/medium business, enterprise) or by region (western markets, eastern markets markets, emerging markets) because market segments tend to start with how their campaign targets users or measures sales conversions.

Personally, I tend to believe that personas are more powerful than market segments for product and campaign creation, but market segmentation is more powerful in execution and measuring the success of what you take to market. Market segmentations often rely on observable characteristics of your audience - where they are and what they do - making it easy for your marketing team to find your target customers and execute. Personas tend to focus on the, often invisible, needs of your audience - what drives their adoption and usage of your offering. And while it's easy to build a product aimed at 'an entrepreneurial moonlighter', it's much harder to quantify and target them in a look-alike audience.

If you are using these two approaches together, I recommend finding an easy way to map how they relate, and understand that the mapping is almost never 1:1 (e.g. software companies in the 'partner' category are likely to employ a mix of 'Einstein's and

'Elvis's; enterprises are likely to employ a mix of 'Mort's and 'Elvis's).

Personas vs user taxonomy attributes

Another common practice is to anchor a target audience on one particular attribute in a user taxonomy, whether it be a role, an industry, or a programming language.

- User roles are most commonly used by engineering groups to call out what job activity is using their product (e.g. 'backend developer', 'web developer', 'mobile app developer').

- Industries (or 'verticals') tend to come into play when there are specific needs, requirements, or behaviors that play out in different types of business (e.g. manufacturing, government, education).

- Programming languages is a pretty self-explanatory grouping (e.g. C++, Java, C#, JavaScript/Node/Angular).

While I believe that user attributes are pretty important for understanding how and where your products are being used, I think that anchoring on these attributes as the way of defining or understanding your audience can put you in an overly-narrow niche. In addition,it tends to turn the focus of your storytelling on product features, rather than thinking about underlying needs that you are looking to satisfy.

Characteristics of a persona

In its simplest form, a persona is a fictional character with a backstory and their own journey to give them depth and to make them interesting to your readers, your engineering and business partners.

If you have a lot of experience, much of this story is based on your intuition and experience with your developers. If you are new to your product's developers, it's time for you to go and either run some focus groups or meet a number of them so that you can start to better understand them, In the basic portrait, I look to include the following details:

- Basic Demographics: To make this person real, give them a name and create a composite of who they are using what you already know about your target developer audience, perhaps anchoring on someone you met at a recent event that you think well represents your user base: what is their age? Where do they live? Where do they work?

- Customer Journey: Now dig in further on what you know about your developers (such as discussions, customers meetings, focus groups, or surveys): How does the developer's world interface with your product or platform? What does their journey generally look like as they move through their world, and as they make contact with yours? Depending on your audience and how established your offering is, this can be either a basic view on their journey as an individual (Past → present → future), or take the shape more of a traditional adoption funnel (Background → awareness → engagement → adoption → advocacy).

- Motivations and aspirations: What drives this individual? Why do they do what they do? What motivates them? What inspires them? Who inspires them? Where do they want to go?

- Pain points and fears: Again - go back to their drive, but from the opposite angle. What keeps them up at night? What do they dread? What do they fear? What are their blind-spots (known or unknown; professional or personal)?

With a basic portrait of our developer, I start to dig into this fictitious character and explore two additional characteristics that create the story of their journey:

Inflection points (adoption triggers): What are the major moments in their life as it relates to your offering? What moves them to the point of making a change? And what is the process for exploring that change?

Adoption facilitators: What can you do for these personas? I tend to break this out into at least three organizational 'calls to action' ('CTAs') - engineering, programs and offers, and marketing - to say "what you can do to help 'Bob'" and provide 1-3 very clear and crisp CTAs on what we can do to help this developer to minimize their pain points and attain their aspirations.

Backing it with data - general demographics, social graphs

Once you have your basic character story written out, then you're ready to flesh it out with market trend data and facts. This helps you round out your persona and refine the portrait away from anecdotal stories, and ground your character in the real world. To do this, I turn to survey data and syndicated research that summarizes larger market trends around my audience.

At this point you may be saying - hold up - why are we only now pulling in market trends and data? Where did all the other stuff come from, if not from data? Well, let's return to how we defined a persona, as a "representation of the goals and behavior" of a group - we are starting with what we know about the internal drivers of our audience, rather than their outputs or observable behaviors. If we started with the market data to define our grouping, we would be doing a market segmentation.

A sample collection of developer personas

In 2012, I set out to build my first collection of personas, the ones mentioned at the start of this chapter. I was doing developer marketing for Windows Phone at the time, and the team built out five personas as shorthand for the mobile developers in the market at the time:

- 'Ravi' worked at a large company that wanted their brand present in mobile, but weren't a mobile company. Although technical, he was business minded and always considered ROI in any mobile investment.

- 'Jerry' worked at a small, mobile-first company that was striving to be ahead of innovation on the platform. He was a developer by background, and in mobile for the excitement. He knew what he was a good at (coding) and was keenly aware of what he wasn't great at (business).

- 'Lana' was part of a team of mobile developers, either as a team member or as a team lead - but filled a number of roles in her day-to-day that would be divided across folks in larger application or web site teams. She was passionate about her role, was ambitious, and was most concerned about the productivity of her and her team.

- 'Tyler' was our mobile moonlighter, passionately building an app in the evenings and weekends. Although he wasn't doing mobile development for a living (often due to a lack of original IP or a business plan), he felt personally committed to his apps and his users.

- 'Nate' was our mobile hobbyist, dabbling in mobile development to experiment or learn, but he didn't invest any significant effort in what he's built.

It's important to note that the mobile space has changed a lot since the early years, but the above represents the state of western mobile development in the early days. The personas themselves also evolved over the years, matching both the changing times and the changing needs of the marketing group, as we targeted developer building for PCs, Xbox, web, IoT, and mixed reality devices.

The persona work in 2012 was built on a foundation of a few years of audience understanding work, both qualitative and quantitative in nature. And we invested an additional year of persona-specific research, talking to almost a hundred developers across the United States and Western Europe to understand why they did what they did. The persona research format was also my personal favorite - we interviewed developers in peer pairs (also known as 'dyads') with such questions as 'if you were a developer super-hero, what would your power be? And who would be your sidekick?' The facilitator we used for the work had a lot of fun with the discussions, and it helped to disarm an otherwise guarded group of developers and uncover some brilliant psychological gems.

For these personas, I'd like to call out a few interesting elements that add texture to the model:

- Developers can, and often will, inhabit multiple personas - I've seen lots of devs who were a 'Ravi' or 'Lana' for work, but a 'Tyler' or 'Nate' at night or on the weekend as they experimented with new technologies or platforms.

- These mobile developer personas held for both app and game developers, which was a constant topic for debate in the company. We focused on the personal drivers of individuals and we found that their personal goals and challenges were similar, even though the technology, workbacks, and team roles differed between app developers and games developers. At the time, the similarity held both within the small organisation/team level ('Jerry') and at the large company level ('Ravi') because most large game studios (e.g. Square Enix) thought of mobile games as an extensions of their console/PC offerings (much as Facebook, at the time, thought of their mobile apps as an extension of their desktop browser based experience).

- Similarly, the personas held across Eastern and Western developer shops. When we went to Asia, we had to create variants for our 'Jerry' and 'Tyler' persona to address differing personal and cultural drives, but the core of the personas held.

To help make our personas useful, we created a number of reference materials to flesh them out: we created landing page for the content and an overview PowerPoint presentation to introduce our five developers (in full slide form and a recording of the presentation of the slides), a dedicated slide deck for each of the five personas, and some additional deliverables for our three marketing-focus personas (the platform decision makers - 'Ravi', 'Jerry', and 'Tyler').

One of the additional deliverables was a wall poster for each of our three focus personas. As you can see from the snapshot of the upper half of Jerry's persona poster, the poster tried to bring the persona to life (digression: Jerry's image is actually a lead mobile developer at the time - to get a real developer vibe, we traded professional headshots for a release form that provided photo usage rights). We blended personal information, actual quotes from actual mobile developers, and market trend data (e.g. platform adoption trends for that persona from analysts such as SlashData, relevant internal survey data, as well as other sources) to bring the persona, and their customer journey, to life.

Meet Jerry

Experienced independent

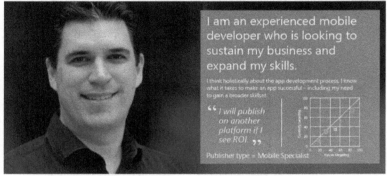

Jerry's journey as an Experienced Independent

On the lower half of the poster, we focused on 'How we can help Jerry', focusing on common concerns we heard from these developers: their motivation, platform selection, team needs, process pain points, what they wanted for their code, and what they wanted for themselves. This half was quite straightforward: the left side brought forth a quote (such as "Speed to market is critical" under 'Process'), while the right side highlighted a corresponding suggestion (such as "Show transparency during certification - get their app out there, so that they can gauge the response and iterate rapidly. Fast publishing process.").

The persona posters were hung in the company's hallways to help our [internal] customer adopt of the team's product (in this case, our research and point-of-view), and also to help the reader feel more informed about the market and our target customer, which allowed them to internalize and use the persona.

Using personas

With personas in hand, let's turn our thinking to usage, both within your group and outside of it. Where and how you use them will vary based on the type of company in which you operate; in our case, some of our engineering partners used them for as the intended 'audience shorthand' within engineering scenarios and product value proposition work but primarily, our personas were used within the developer marketing organization. In fact, my team increasingly used our personas as the core of our marketing efforts over the five years following their inception. I did so many educational presentations on the topic of personas that I'm still known in some parts of Microsoft as 'the Windows persona guy', with reverence by those that bought in, and with an eye roll by those who didn't yet understand the value contained in this approach. That being said, I've also been bought many a drink (whether with alcohol or caffeine) by those who once sighed at the personal concept, but who later found the faith after changing roles or companies!

Marketing agency briefs

When our team engaged with agencies for marketing campaigns or content development, we included a simplified version of our target personas (10-12 slides of the larger deck). Initially, we did this because an agency wanted to know more about the audience, but this quickly became a best practice in our RFP process as it yielded much better campaign pitches on the first try.

Campaign and offer development

If you've done your homework and captured the motivations of your target audience, you can start to use your insights around the customer journey and adoption decisions to build a marketing plan around each audience.

For example, in Windows Phone, we targeted each of our key three personas via different developer marketing motions.

- For 'Ravi' developers, we used our business development teams as part of our larger conversations with the executive decision makers in the business, which was often the key for investments.

- For 'Tyler' developers, we built a gamified developer program with Nokia called DVLUP and engaged at the community level, building a sense of fun and fraternity.

- For 'Jerry' developers, we ran a number of programs and offers that helped both improve their business (design help, business consults, and marketing help) and helped them feel like a bigger fish in our ecosystem.

Developer messaging

Every marketer does messaging a different way. At Microsoft, we generally follow a standard positioning and messaging framework process. This comprises a top-line marketing message for the offering along with three messaging pillars that support it. How you best align your offering's messaging and positioning is well beyond the scope of this chapter, but what I'd like to hit on here is how I used personas to evolve my team's approach to something as structured as a messaging framework.

After a few iterations of the developer messaging for Windows Phone, I tried adapting my approach to create a messaging framework with four variants: a core messaging framework that follows the normal process, but also adding a messaging framework variant that is tailored to each of our key three personas. The approach used three-steps:

1. First, we would do some qualitative testing on our messaging with small groups of developers to understand what they liked, or didn't like, about our top-line developer messaging, both from a conceptual and wording point of view

2. Second, we would also inquire about some of the broader concepts in our offering and probe for areas that either delighted the room or felt like we stepped on a landmine.

3. Third, we adjusted the messaging for audience, potentially swapping messaging order or even sometimes one of the core messages with a brand new one. We would then go back and revisit our core

messaging with the findings and evaluate if we needed to make any changes to the larger framework, as well.

As you go down this path, it's important to approach developer messaging with a growth mindset. For me, it was helpful to work with some professional focus group moderators early on to learn how to enter a discussion with curiosity (rather than trying to correct what may first be seen as a misguided or misinformed opinion) to gather insights on structuring my storytelling to developers.

Platform usability

It's worth noting that developer personas are also useful in evaluating the usability of the platforms we are marketing. When one thinks about how to adopt or position a platform, you most likely think about feature sets and checkboxes - what's present and what's missing. That thinking is about half of the picture - the quantitative half of the picture. Equally important is the qualitative half of the adoption picture - whether that experience was delightful or painful. A recent artifact I've seen is the idea of Friction Analysis in adoption. As we looked at messaging, and we noticed that the different personas experienced the platform differently. This brings us back to 'Mort'/'Elvis'/'Einstein' in how they approach building UI using user controls. Each persona wants something different from the development experience, and each brings their own collection of requirements and biases. For example, 'Mort' wants to quickly lay out his UI visually, and finds UI templates very productive; while 'Elvis' puts a lot of value on the ability to tweak user control properties and override the default behaviors.

By understanding each persona's perspective and assumptions, you can properly build and position a product to that audience. And by sharing a common persona set between marketing and engineering, all of the teams share a common lens for designing and building your product. Particularly when your product can prioritize the audience and be clear in what they want and need, it's much easier to build a product that meets those requirements and delights them.

Tips and tricks: persona creation

So let's turn our discussion to the process of creating personas. As we discussed early in the chapter, personas can be as simple or as complex, and as cheap or as expensive, as you want them to be. In this section, I've pulled together a collection of points that are worth considering as you embark upon the process of creating your personas.

Persona project kick-off day

As you kick off the persona creation, it's critical that you gather up and include all of your extended stakeholders as you launch into persona creation. I've found it critical to include key folks attached to the product - marketing, engineering, and developer relations - to understand what is already known about your audience, and what additional information would help them better meet its needs.

Much like organizing focus groups, I recommend sitting down with stakeholders with aligned purposes and mindsets to make the most of your time. And, much like running a focus group, you may want to use a neutral third-party or facilitator (either external to your company, or just external to your group) to help allay any fears of organizational bias on the part of your stakeholders. In the conversations, you'll want to explore the following:

- How would they use developer personas in their work?
- What do they use today?
- What do they know about their target audience?
- If they had to group your audience into three groups, how would they do it?
- How do they measure success with the developer audience?
- Can they share their last business review on progress with their target audience(s)?

For efficiency, you may want to set up a unified kick-off meeting to set some context for what's coming, when it's coming, and what you want/need out of everyone. This will help you to define the work to be done, and to let everyone know that the work brings together voices and perspectives across the company.

And as you progress, you'll want to communicate across all groups on general project progress - no less frequently than monthly. You'll also want to communicate with each group on progress with any findings as it relates to their questions and/or problems. Don't underestimate the value of having the larger group communications; giving everyone visibility on the left-to-right coverage of the project helps them see the personas through a larger lens than just their own.

Understand your existing customer segmentation

Particularly if you're in product management or developer marketing, it's critical to look at your existing customer segmentation, and how your company goes to market with your company's market segments. As we discussed earlier, there are many ways that you can divide and group an audience, and everyone will have their own way of slicing and dicing the group.

For your personas to take root in the business, you'll need to speak the language of your business and be able to express how you go to market with your personas. If you can't frame your personas that way, you will spend a lot of your time fighting the existing model and trying to explain how persona 'a' maps into segment 'b', or risk all of your work becoming shelf-ware. Returning to the original goal for your personas, they need to advance your organization by aligning goals and audience across the company.

Talk to your target customers and understand their story

As you build your personas, don't spend all of your time behind one-way glass. While funded research has its place in the effort, it's critical to get to know developers by going where they are and observing them in their natural habitat:

- Visit them in their work environment. As you build out your personas, drop in and chat with your developer audience to understand what they do and why they do it where they are. And while you're there, take some pictures for the reports. To find some local developers while you're out on business travel, you can reach out via LinkedIn or just connect with a few via your engineering or developer relations team. If they're customers or partners, they would love to have you drop by.

- Talk to them at events. While you're at a relevant event, hang out at your booth, or break your chains and walk the floor, introducing yourself and getting to know those around you. It may feel odd at first, but you'll be surprised at the conversations you'll have at an event. It's a great way to get an unprompted view of your company, the market, and what's on their mind. Those attending paid to go to that event, after all, so they must be invested in the topic.

Storming and norming

After you've come to understand what your business needs and what your developer audience wants, it's time to get to creative and iterate, iterate, iterate. This portion of the process is much more black art than science, but a few things that work for me:

- Sticky notes: I love writing down everything I think is interesting in the 'Characteristics of a persona' section of this chapter. Then start looking for commonalities, much like a quant-based cluster analysis...except this is all stuff in their head.

- 3 question gearbox: As you start to get to your groupings, see if you can define 3-5 characteristics that define that group. These characteristics would be the 3 survey questions that you place in a survey or event registration to understand which personas you're reaching, or the messaging you want to test. For my mobile developer personas, it was around (1) why they did it (pure hobby; moonlighting; profit), (2) size of team/company, and (3) decision making authority.

- Granularity: You generally don't want too many personas to represent your audience. You should push to simplify and collapse groups where you can, but keep it granular enough to be useful.

- Test it: Lastly, build out a composite of your persona(s) and test it out with your stakeholders and with your work deliverables. If it helps and moves things forward - awesome! If it doesn't - it's time to iterate!

Always be hustling

Once you have your personas in hand, the work doesn't stop. Much like your engineering partners, you have a minimal viable product, so ship that thing and start hustling and iterating to drive constant improvement.

Internal promotion

Don't underestimate what goes into marketing your work internally, whether you work in a small company or a big one - folks either adopt your work or it becomes shelf-ware, locked away in some file folder or abandoned on an island of misfit toys. For me, the posters and monthly presentations on the topic helped a lot. But your mileage will vary.

Cultural refinement

Once you build and ship your initial product (remember - always be shipping), check it for unconscious bias and/or sample bias. In my case, we built our personas based on US and Western European experience and data points. The following year, we tested it in Asia (in China, India, Japan, and Korea) and found interesting cultural differences anchored in such things as community interactions and career movement. As one example, we found that in China, particularly in Tier 1 cities, most developers were less interested in taking risks on new or radically different platforms, for fear of hurting their trajectory out of programming and into management.

As necessary, tweak your personas or make notes within them on how to execute your marketing campaigns according to local area or audience variations.

Always be learning

Lastly, the tech industry is always changing. You (and your personas) should be prepared to change with it. Always bring a growth mindset to your work and assume that everything you do should be reviewed annually to see if you're still in touch with the market your developers represent.

- As part of your marketing post-mortems (for events, campaigns, and releases), evaluate whether you landed your product with your target persona(s). Did you reach your target developers? And, on the flip side, did the developers you reach properly represent your personas? In our case, our 'Jerry' persona changed a lot in its first year of life, going from teams of 1-2 to 1-5, and going from an entrepreneurial focused developer to one of empowerment.

- Stay out there with your audience, attending at least 2-3 developer events per year - and remember that your own events don't count! Much like you did when you built the personas, talk to your developers and ensure that you still have the pulse of your community. And if you sense that sentiment or motivations are shifting within your audience, it's time to revisit.

- Finally, stay up on your industry trends and be sure that your team thoroughly reevaluates your personas every 2-3 years to see if your groupings still hold. Although some groupings can be evergreen (Mort/Elvis/Einstein), the mobile developer personas in this chapter are definitely dated and no longer effective...you don't want your marketing programs to feel like syndicated television reruns from ten years ago. By continually checking the industry perspective, it helps prevent you from living in a bubble if your audience is getting more and more niche.

Over time, you'll probably come to think of your personas as a set of close virtual friends, just as I did. Just remember to enjoy your time with them while you have it and be ready to let them go as the world takes you down different paths!

Chapter 2 | Successful Developer Email Marketing

Desiree Motamedi: Head of Developer Marketing - Facebook

Throughout this chapter, you'll learn about Facebook's developer marketing journey in relation to email; from our challenges and insights on how to solve them, to best practices, audience insights, and where we see email marketing headed in the future. Development is about improving technology and moving forward. It is not a one-way street - we're all building together. We apply this mindset to our marketing to tailor our messaging to the audience and give them what they want and need.

Introduction

Email has been around for decades and is used by billions of people around the world as a way to rapidly exchange electronic messages. As a fast, free tool, it seems only natural that marketing has used it since its early days to connect with people. In 1978, Gary Thuerk, a Marketing Manager at Digital Equipment Corp sent what is considered the first mass email. It was a marketing message promoting the company's machines to several hundred people over the pre-Internet network, Arpanet. The results were impressive, generating more than $13 million in sales for the company. Email marketing was born! (Source: ComputerWorld https://sdata.me/CljUnz)

Much has changed in the 40 years since 1978. Checking email on a computer is no longer the primary way people communicate online. In fact, according to data collected and analysed by Litmus Software, more email is read on mobile than on desktop email clients, with 47% of email opened on a mobile device (Source: "The 2017 Email Client Market Share," Jan 2018 https://sdata.me/DBAJQu). Furthermore, a recent study revealed that mobile email conversion rates have caught up to desktop conversions, with both at an average of 3.3 percent for the year. (Source: MarketingLand, March 2018 https://sdata.me/kKMYpa).

With 72 percent of consumers in Litmus' 2016 State of Email report stating that email is their first choice for brand communication, and more than 225 billion emails sent every day (a 5 percent increase from previous years), email continues to play an important role in brands' marketing strategies.

To stand out from the crowd, marketers have to blend creativity with data, tailoring their content to be relevant to their audience and reaching them at the right time, in the right place. And if you're working in developer marketing, you have a particular challenge because traditionally, developers hate marketing. They want communication to be authentic and useful. Keeping that in mind, it's essential to take an honest look at developer email marketing and ask tough questions, such as:

Will the reader think we're trying to sell them something?
Are we using a developer-driven approach?
Are we pushing our products or services rather than creating value and trust?

It's more important than ever to get this right today, with so many companies vying for developers' attention.

No one taught me about developers

As the Head of Developer Product Marketing at Facebook, a significant portion of my job entails understanding how developers think, what makes them tick, what keeps them up at night, and how Facebook can ultimately help them do their work better. Over the course of two decades, I've gotten to know this demographic inside and out through a plethora of go-to-market strategies that my teams have helped build and execute.

Through it all, there have been no rulebooks or guidelines on how to specifically target this demographic. There was no *"How to Market Facebook's Products to Developers for Dummies."* Through endless hard work, a ton of trial and error, and the support of fantastic marketing teams, we've begun to understand how to fine-tune our message to developers. However, the nature of this particular demographic is that it's constantly changing to keep up with such a fast-paced industry.

A little more about my work with developers prior to Facebook — I began my career in Silicon Valley with Adobe and spent over eight years as Group Product Marketing Manager, where I oversaw several product launches, including the Adobe Flash Media Server family of products and the repackaging of Creative Suite.

Understanding developers had never been more important than when I began my tenure at Google as their Product Marketing Lead for mobile apps. At Google, I was responsible for "rolling thunder" marketing strategies, which build momentum and generate buzz to get the audience wondering 'what's coming?' before a public announcement. My team worked to build a vibrant developer ecosystem around the Mobile App Ads Platform, which includes AdMob, AdWords, and Google Analytics. I've carried over the learnings from that experience to my current role at Facebook, where I head up global developer marketing efforts.

I love working with and nurturing relationships with developers. It's fascinating and fun working with this diverse audience who are having such a profound impact on our world today.

Facebook's developer platform

Most people think of Facebook as a social media site, connecting people with their family and friends, as well as businesses. It's a place to share content, send messages, and interact with the people you care about.

But Facebook is more than that. We launched our developer platform at the F8 conference in May 2007, enabling developers to build software for people on Facebook, with tools and features to help them grow. At the time, Facebook's user base was 20 million people. Today, we're at more than 2 billion users, and we present developers around the world with the opportunity to connect with even more people.

Just as our consumer audience has grown, our developer ecosystem has expanded and evolved over the years. To achieve this scale, we have seen some organic growth. However, that's just one part of the equation.

To grow the developer ecosystem, our task in the Developer Marketing Team is to connect with and drive developers to adopt our products. We do this by using engaging content that keeps them coming back to us. We craft content, messaging, and campaigns with our end-goal of product adoption in mind. We plan email campaigns, newsletters, websites like developers.facebook.com, social postings, and more to get developers' attention.

To drive success, we've tried and tested different marketing approaches, built out a robust suite of tools, and fostered community through a variety of programs and events. Recently, we've invested heavily in forming a full-funnel marketing initiative, which involves a solid email marketing strategy aimed at engaging our developer audience. Throughout the process, our North Star has been to track and measure results, collect data across platforms and use what we've learned along the way to optimize going forward.

It's all about the data

In early 2017, we decided to ramp up our email marketing to developers, creating a full-funnel approach that ties all campaigns back to building awareness, influencing consideration, driving adoption, and increasing retention for a loyal audience. To achieve this, we aimed to accurately measure every interaction, optimizing accordingly and mapping out an ideal strategy for growth. We asked ourselves "Did that article in our last email newsletter actually drive sign-ups?", "How many of our subscribers click through?", "Did that specific newsletter article drive adoption of the product?". We wanted to discover which approaches worked, which content had the most impact, and how to keep developers engaged over time. But setting ourselves up for success wasn't easy...

First, we had to decide which CRM we would use. We had to consider functionality, support, ability to integrate with Salesforce, reporting features, data collection, scalability, and more. After weighing the options, having conducted our own research and speaking with other teams using CRMs, we landed on Marketo as the best choice for us.

To get started with our CRM, Marketo, we knew we had to pipe over our developer data that existed elsewhere, because we wanted a complete view of our audience's behavior from one centralized location. It was crucial that we not lose any of the existing collected data about our developer audience. The result was a complete database of developer signals including product adoption, online behavior, and who they are. We had gathered this existing information through tracking across our website, social channels, email campaigns, paid media, events, and third-party sites. It was important to us that we didn't lose it - it's marketing gold, after all!

To move this trove of data points into our new system, we had to enlist the help of our Engineering and IT teams. We needed coordinated resources to get the data cleanly piped in and organized in a way that would make it meaningful and accessible. Overall, integrating our data and syncing up Marketo with Salesforce took us about 6 months with the help of numerous teams. It was worth the effort to capture registration details and interests in one place, but it took some serious time and cooperation! From contact information to product adoption, page views on our websites, and more, our engineers had their work cut out for them.

With this first substantial hurdle out of the way, we would be able to build a solid email marketing strategy. With vast amounts of data, we would be able to personalize our content, connecting with our audience in a more meaningful way.

Testing, testing, 1,2,3

After successfully moving all of our data to Marketo, we set out to create a variety of email campaigns. From trigger-based to batch, we tested a slew of different approaches across content, layout, design, messaging, send day and time, and more. But consistent throughout these tests was our measurement. Tracking performance is the key to success. Equally as important is having benchmarks and goals in place to see how you're improving. To get started, do a quick online search for industry standards for delivery, open rates, and click-throughs. CRMs such as HubSpot, Mailchimp, and Marketo will periodically publish current benchmarks that you can use as a guide. Use these as a starting point, then set your own goals. Remember, the numbers shouldn't change - you need a constant to measure yourself against.

For us, we set the bar high, aiming to achieve 15-22% open rate and 1.5-2.5% click-throughs. We have kept this number and now track our performance week-over-week and month-over-month. Looking at our reports over time, we keep a lookout for any trends or red flags. Did we see a high number of unsubscribes with a particular email? Was the open rate higher on a Tuesday send? Are more people engaging with videos than articles? These are the kinds of things we monitor, and we use our findings to improve for the next send.

Pulling the trigger

With email marketing, you have the opportunity for personalization and advanced targeting to help drive awareness and adoption.

Trigger-based campaigns are based on customer interactions with your content (e.g. subscription, page visits, product adoption). They help to drive people through the funnel in a very personalized way. With these campaigns, you can map out the customer journey more precisely and make decisions based on real data. What brought them to your content? Did they take action after your first email? Did your reminder emails drive them to conversion? How many times did you 'touch' them before they adopted your product?

For nurture campaigns, all email sends are automated and are based on the actions a lead takes. To prepare for this flow, we had to map out the potential journey and actions we wanted leads to take. From there, we mapped out the potential outcomes of action/inaction and created emails according to each one. Then, we piped data into our CMS and had the logic built out to correspond with the potential developer journeys - all aiming to drive product adoption. Trigger-based campaigns are definitely not simple, but they are worth it because you gain a better understanding of the unique journey each person takes on their path to conversion. These campaigns also help to showcase which points along the way are successfully driving action, and which ones are not. This is extremely valuable insight, and it can help you make decisions to optimize the path to conversion.

The welcome nurture flow

Once a developer registers on developers.facebook.com, he or she gets added to our database. From there, we look at whether or not the developer has created an app so that we can send them one of two welcome emails.

If the developer has already created an app ID with us, they receive "Welcome Email A" with next steps and a welcome to the platform. From there, we wait 24 hours to see if the developer adopts a product. If they do, then we add them to the nurture stream for authentication services and send a prompt to adopt either our Analytics offering or another one of our products. If they haven't adopted a product, then we send two more email prompts encouraging them - one is sent immediately, and the other after 48 hours. If nothing happens after 120 hours, then we mark the lead inactive in the database and filter the type of material we send them (mostly platform updates and nothing product-specific).

If the developer hasn't created an app, they'll receive "Welcome Email B" with next steps, demonstrating platform value and encouraging them to create an App ID. In the first 96 hours they'll receive three prompts from us to create an app - the first is sent after 24 hours, second at 48 hours, and the third after 96 hours. If 130 hours go by and there's still no activity from the developer, then we mark lead inactive in the database.

Newsletter

Along this journey, we've made some amazing strides and have tested and learned from a variety of experiences, good and bad. The Facebook for Developers newsletter campaigns have been full of valuable lessons.

Our newsletters enable us to actively re-engage with our developer audience on a monthly basis, providing updates on our platform and products. We experiment with different layouts, different times of day for send, subject line AB tests, different types of content, and content length, etc. - tweaking and refining the content each month for the most significant impact.

We've also added "Share With a Friend" functionality to enable those who have subscribed to send the email to others they think may be interested. This helps us to grow our database organically.

Along the way, we've hit some bumps in the road. We used trial and error to outline a clear process for approvals, learning from each month's send what worked and what didn't. We also asked "Where did we experience delays, and what can we do to make it smoother for next time?". We also had to evaluate deliverability across devices, email service providers, and more. Other questions we asked were "Is what we're seeing on our screen the same thing someone on a different screen will see?", and "How can we make sure the experience is consistent?". Through it all, learning is key - take what you've experienced and apply it to the next version so that you're constantly improving.

It's not always an easy road to success

Although we've had great success in many ways, there have been several obstacles we've had to overcome along the way.

Technology was a challenge for us at times. Integrating Marketo and Salesforce is great when they play nicely together. However, this is not always the case. From segmenting developers by product adoption, to segmenting users into buckets by developer vs. business, it can be hard to draw a line and determine the best approach. There are many different types of people with different backgrounds and interests, so it can be hard to figure out the best way to segment them. We are lucky to have a dedicated data analyst who is able to sift through all of this information and help us to glean key insights from the data we collected. Combined with email AB testing, the insights from our data analyst help us to better understand our audience. While you may not be able to have a full-time data analyst on staff, I highly recommend you have someone who can look at all of the data you're collecting and make actionable recommendations for your marketing team.

Another challenge was determining the logic for email campaigns. It is very detailed/intricate, and all potential outcomes need to be considered. We had to go through many rounds of review and feedback about timing and content in order to align on how we thought we could drive the most product adoption through the nurture email streams.

The insights you receive about your audience based on the data you collect makes all of the efforts and obstacles worthwhile. You can get the complete picture of a person's journey to conversion, and it gives you an inside look at what marketing approaches are working, as well as what could be improved. Marketing is only as good as its data. The more you know about your audience, what's working, and what's not, the higher your return on investment.

Keep these best practices in mind for your own campaigns

Team organization

It takes a strong team to build out a robust email marketing strategy. In our case, we needed technical expertise in the form of engineers with deep knowledge of Marketo and Salesforce. We also needed product and audience insights from our product marketing managers so that we could create tailored campaigns based on our findings. In addition, we needed specialists to execute and report on our email campaigns. Plus, we needed someone - or better yet, a team of people - who could understand all of it and see the bigger picture.

For each of our team members, we ask "What are their strengths?" and "What are their weaknesses?". I consider who should take on each role, and set them up for success, because when everyone gets to play to his or her strengths and work together, great things happen. A "unicorn" who understands both the developer audience and full-funnel marketing will be very hard to find! When I hired someone to handle our email marketing, I set out to find an individual who understood the full funnel marketing approach. It didn't necessarily matter whether or not they were familiar with the developer audience because we could support them to learn over time, and onboard them by interfacing with cross-functional teams, encouraging conversations with developers and product teams both in-house and out in the world.

However, it is also important to have people on your team who have a technical understanding. They don't have to be developers themselves, but they should know what they're talking about and understand what drives the developer community. They need to understand developers' challenges and know how to communicate effectively. For example, it's important not to add a lot of "fluff" text when communicating with developers. Say what you need to say succinctly, and don't add a huge lead-up with background information. No matter what news you're sharing with developers, make sure you deliver it straight and to the point.

Stakeholders

When developing your operational process you should keep your stakeholders and team members in mind. You should be asking " Who needs to sign off on this?" and "Who will your email marketing program impact within your company?

Make sure to keep stakeholders actively involved and up-to-date, so everyone is on the same page. Send them the items you need their sign-off on, and make sure you get approvals when you need them! To streamline your projects, set up a process for incoming requests and clarify who needs to receive the initial details and next steps. Outline it all in a clear process with timelines to help manage expectations. Of course there will be times when campaigns need to be rushed (last minute emergencies can always come up), but try to plan ahead whenever possible so no one gets burned out. This will help them to absorb new information as it comes, which will happen, quickly and often. The more organized and structured the plan, the better!

Test your messaging

Run a subject line AB test using different phrasing in each and see which one gets more engagement. Strong calls to action are key. Developers want information clearly and succinctly presented to them, so your call to action should be very clear and stand out from the rest of your email. For example, our recent email subject line mentioning GDPR was a big loser, since the audience was inundated with GDPR alerts that week. Even though the information was useful to developers, a subject line featuring one of the other articles would have had better open rates that month.

Another example is our standard developer newsletter subject line. In the past, we would always make the subject line "Facebook for Developers Newsletter" followed by the month. We saw that open rates weren't what we wanted them to be, so we ran a subject line AB test. We found that including a sneak peek of the content featured in the email was much more successful. Since then, we've used this subject line structure to help drive open rates.

Be conversational

Developers are generally averse to the most common marketing techniques, especially sales-y lingo and jargon. For example, avoid words like "enhance," "robust," or "special". In general, it's best not to overuse adjectives when describing something. We've found that it's best to keep information short and sweet - be straightforward and informative. Clearly present your information and highlight key benefits. It's best to showcase your information in a problem > solution fashion.

This goes for any email, but for developers especially, avoid spammy techniques. Limit your exclamation points, keep capitalization consistent, and avoid embedding forms within the body of your email. Also be sure not to send too many emails. While "too many" is subjective and depends on your audience's interests, be sure to keep an eye on your unsubscribes, which will give you an indication if you're overdoing it. In general, we try not to send more than 4 emails per month to the same people. No matter how useful the email may be, no one likes having their inbox inundated with messages from the same company.

Product update emails should be short and to-the-point. This way the email gets to the heart of the issue quickly. Have calls to action about where to learn more or whom to contact for questions. This keeps the audience engaged and informed.

Test your layout

We recently redesigned our developer website. This new design, of course, needed to carry over into all developer-facing content, which involved redesigning our newsletters and emails. We saw this as an opportunity to see what types of content layout our audience prefers - so we ran a test. We revamped our existing newsletter, simply updating the logo, colors and font, but keeping the structure the same. Then, we created a brand new layout, shortening content sections, updating logos, colors, fonts, content types, and more. We used both, sending half of our mailing list one layout, while the other half received the all-new design. This is an excellent way to determine how to connect with your audience. Do they prefer short, bite-sized blurbs, or do they want meaty articles within their email? Do they like clickable images, or would they rather have text links? Try it out! See what sticks.

Test date/time of send

What day of the week results in the best open rates and engagement? What time of day performs better? Are you sending to different regions in different time zones? These are all things to keep in mind when considering effective timing of an email campaign.

Additionally, see what your competitors are doing, and try and find something that sets your offering apart. Don't get lost in the noise.

Track online and offline interactions

For events, send invites to your target audience via your CRM. Target your audience based on region, product interest/adoption, activity, etc. Once someone signs up, have an automatic confirmation email lined up to send to them upon form completion. Collect info on who attends and doesn't attend your event and send them follow-ups accordingly (thank you notes to attendees, sorry we missed you to no-shows). You can then use all of this data in campaigns in the future - using data about who attended an event as part of target criteria.

Think globally

Offer content in other languages/tailored to different regions. Don't just rely on direct translations, though. There are nuances between regions that will need to be taken into account for your audience to hear your authentic voice. For example, we only send our newsletter in English because the content we link to is generally only in English. We plan to localize our nurture campaigns into other languages, however, since that is static content that can be tailored to region more easily. Work with people in-region to localize your content. For Facebook, the majority of our developers are outside of the US so this is a major ongoing effort for us.

Build deeper relationships with your audience

To make email content relevant and helpful to our developer audience, we listened to our active developer database. Did they have feedback about our tools or messaging? Were the resources we sent them valuable? Through surveys, we were able to get their feedback and plan accordingly to make our emails more useful.

Showing that you are listening is important. Give your audience the mic and absorb their feedback so you can give them what they want. Hear their concerns, their questions, their preferences and use it to provide them with valuable content they're going to enjoy or find useful.

At Facebook, many of our development tools are open source, and we are a company built by developers for developers. So prioritizing feedback from the developer community across channels is key for us. By hearing what they have to say in groups, forums, social media, at events, and more, we're able to discover key takeaways that we can turn into actionable items for our marketing.

Understand the full path to conversion

To understand the journey, it's more than just measuring opens, click-through rates, and link engagement. We also need to understand how developers came into our database. Did they fill out a form for an event? Did they visit our website and sign up? Were they on a social channel and came to us that way? It's crucial to measure the full journey and compile this attribution data, overlaid with our findings about messaging/content, formats, subject lines, image style, different calls to action, and more. The more data you can pull together the better you can ultimately serve that developer's needs.

So what's next for us?

We've seen 1.8M developers download our SDKs and APIs - so it looks like something we're doing is working. Our database has grown to 3M developers, and we're going to be expanding into new regions, and marketing to developers in other parts of the world even more effectively.

For us, localization is our next white whale. We have an established global audience, and we want to do more to better connect with our developers around the world by offering email content in their language of choice. Localization is more than translations though - we also want content that is suited to each region/locale so that it's more relevant.

Lead scoring is also on the horizon for our team. Some leads are more valuable than others - engaging more, converting, demonstrating higher open/clicks. We want to have an at-a-glance view at who these people are so we can weed out those who aren't actively involved and focus more on these "higher scoring" leads. But for this, we need a system and built out criteria. It will take some planning! I'll update you about our progress in the next Essential Guide.

Chapter 3 | The Power Of Community

Jacob Lehrbaum: Vice President of Developer and Admin Relations - Salesforce

In today's connected world it seems like everything has a developer service, such as an API, an SDK, or a platform. This is because the apps and devices that brands and software developers are creating become significantly more valuable when they can share data or services with each other, or can be extended by a developer with a great idea. For example, in my digital home, I can control my Nest thermostat, my Hue lights, and even my Wemo-powered Christmas tree with my Amazon Alexa. By harnessing the creativity of the world-wide developer population, vendors are seeing their products extended and adopted in ways they never thought possible.

But simply creating a developer service is not enough to declare victory. Unless you have an incredibly differentiated offering, you are often one of multiple options out there that developers can choose from. This is where community can become such a powerful factor in your success. Developers, by their very nature, are builders who create things that are entirely new. And in the process of creating things that are new, they often use your services in ways that you didn't anticipate and this is where community comes in. With a vibrant community, you will have

47

developers sharing best practices with each other, helping solve challenging problems, and even sharing code to help everyone go faster. When developers see a service with a rich community around it, they are also more confident in adopting it! But community does not happen overnight - it requires focus, investment, nurturing, and patience.

Introduction

While communities can form organically, planning can turn your community into a rocket-ship. Communities exist because people grow to be passionate about your product or technology, and if you have a thoughtful program for sharing guidelines, tools and templates with developers, you will amplify their efforts in a way that will make the entire community stronger. And championing their success creates a positive feedback loop that inspires others to follow in their footsteps.

When thinking about your community, it's important to remember that they do not work for you - they are free to participate and contribute as much or as little as they wish. They may disengage if you don't meet their needs or if they feel like the community is not welcoming or inclusive. For this reason, it's critical for your community program to be helpful and to focus on their success instead of your own, internal objectives. Know how building a community supports your goals, but focus on being helpful and let the rest follow. Because it will, and your community will be stronger for it.

I've had the privilege of working with four communities over nearly 20 years in the developer tools and platforms industry: Linux, Java, Ruby-on-Rails and most recently, and currently, the Salesforce community. These communities have been incredibly varied ranging from open source with Linux and Ruby-on-Rails to industry-standard with Java, and finally company-specific with Salesforce. But in each and every community, I've been struck by the passion of the members and their genuine care for helping their fellow developers succeed.

In this chapter on the power of community, we'll explore how you can bring people together to promote organic connections and collaboration, pave a path for your community members that aligns to your goals, make your community members feel and act like insiders, discover and champion community leaders to empower your most engaged advocates, and measure your success within your company to ensure that your community efforts get the funding and recognition they deserve.

Bringing people together

Community culture

Community is fundamentally about people coming together to help each other, and the first step is to create a community that people want to belong to. A big part of that is your product itself, but there are things you can do above and beyond your product to make your community be a place that people want to spend time. One of the ways you can do that is through culture.

At Salesforce, a fundamental part of our culture is giving back. As Marc Benioff has said, "the business of business is improving the state of the world." In fact, Salesforce was founded on the 1:1:1 model which dedicated 1% of Salesforce's equity, 1% of Salesforce's product and 1% of Salesforce employees' time back to communities around the world. For this reason, we've made giving back a big part of our events and messaging, and we see the community adopting this as well! A great example of this is Surf Force, a Salesforce community-led conference in the UK that, in addition to learning about Salesforce, features surfing and a beach clean-up. It might sound a little weird, but the attendees absolutely rave about it, and it gets an incredible, international audience.

Another part of our culture is to have fun and be inspirational, which results in stronger bonds across our community as well as an approachable feel. We do this through playful copywriting, highlighting the success of people and groups across our community, incorporating fun programs into our events and campaigns like our #OhanaFriday hashtag on Twitter, as well as a family of mascots that includes Astro who believes that anyone can be anything they want to be, as well as Codey the Bear, Cloudy the Goat, Metamoose, Appy Camper, and our original mascot, SaaSy.

By combining our core values, we've seen a culture develop across our community of developers that has strengthened our community.

Once you have created a community that people want to belong to, there are a number of ways that you can help your community come together, including but not limited to developer group meetups for getting together in real life and online channels such as social media, Slack / IRC, Online Q&A and hosted discussion groups.

Developer groups

From my perspective, developer groups are one of the most fundamental components of a successful developer community. This is because having an in-person support network is invaluable whether you are just getting started, or looking to skill-up. Nothing beats being able to talk to a real human being. The people that choose to lead these groups are some of your most important allies and you need to treat them like an extended part of your team (more on this later) and give them what they need to be successful. Every company has access to different resources, but consider whether you can help with refreshments, physical space, marketing, content, or access to your experts. For example, at Salesforce we'll reimburse community group leaders up to a fixed amount per meeting. We also have an unofficial policy to ensure that our developer evangelists and product managers visit local groups whenever they are nearby, and we provide access to sessions, including slide decks and videos, from our major events so they can deliver them at their local groups.

Whether you create your own developer group program or identify and support existing developer groups will depend on the size of your community. For example, Sun, as the creator and steward of the Java Platform, was able to build and grow a substantial developer group program called Java User Groups (JUGs) and while the torch has passed to Oracle, there are still over 200 JUGs in existence today. At Salesforce, we have over 236 developer groups in 56 countries.

On the other hand, during my time at Engine Yard, we instead chose to support existing open source communities such as Ruby on Rails and PHP. Given the open-source nature of Engine Yard's platform-as-a-service, their users identified more as members of these existing open source communities. We used Engine Yard's offices in San Francisco, Portland, and Dublin to host meetup groups for those communities and others free of charge, and even paid for pizza and beer! By supporting adjacent communities, Engine Yard was seen as a sponsor and leader.

As you think about your developer group strategy, think about how your users identify and where they spend their time. If your product is part of their identity, think about creating your own groups. If your users identify as part of multiple communities, perhaps start by supporting those existing community groups and defer the decision on whether to create your own groups.

Online channels

Even if you have hundreds of developer groups arranging meetups, few companies, if any, have groups everywhere they are needed, and most meetup groups meet monthly at best. We live in an increasingly global world, and bringing people together via online channels like Twitter, Facebook, Reddit, StackExchange or Slack is an excellent way to keep the community humming 24 hours a day and 365 days a year. Why so many channels you may ask? We've found that developers want to learn in many different ways, so we like to meet them where they are and support organic efforts that spring naturally out of the community.

At Salesforce, we manage our Twitter and Facebook accounts directly, with active community participation. For example, on Twitter, we have a hashtag called #askforce that is monitored by community leaders around the globe, where you can ask for help with issues you may encounter.

The Salesforce StackExchange was created by community members and continues to be managed by the community. In addition to the Salesforce StackExchange, we also have developer forums that we host on developer.salesforce.com, moderated by 2-3 full-time Salesforce employees, a number of Salesforce product managers and a handful of carefully selected community volunteers. Each month, the StackExchange and the forums receive participation from thousands in the community, which is split in terms of its preference. Why do we continue to support both? We've found that our first-party developer forums tend to be more forgiving for new entrants to our community and a good complement to the Salesforce StackExchange.

Closing the circle with the meetup groups, we also provide online discussion groups powered by Salesforce Community Cloud, so that individual communities can engage together, with both private and public settings depending on the sensitivity of the discussion topic. In addition to online homes for each of our developer groups, community members have created groups for big Salesforce events like Dreamforce and TrailheaDX for our products, specific industries, women in tech, diversity and much more. What is special about these groups is that while we provide the infrastructure, it is our community members that create (and sustain) so many of these groups.

Pave the path

Communities are made up of people. People who have a wide range of skills, goals, and perspectives, and who are participating in the community of their own free will, not for a paycheck. Many of the best contributions I've seen from the community are organic in nature, and are nothing we could have planned, anticipated or even suggested!

Community members will see opportunities in their own local communities and come up with amazing solutions that couldn't have been anticipated. Within the Salesforce community, we have countless examples, such as members who have created their own podcasts and blogs. There are over two-dozen community-led conferences such as Midwest Dreamin' and Snowforce. The community have launched a Speaker Academy to help first-time speakers get talks accepted at conferences such as Dreamforce. We have also seen the community rally in a big way around a grassroots organization called PepUpTech, which is striving to address the disproportionate numbers of underrepresented groups in tech by helping people get jobs in the Salesforce ecosystem.

You don't need to be entirely hands-off. Guidelines, best practices, resources, and templates can help you pave a path towards the outcome you want. Let's say a member of your community wants to create a developer group. They could certainly do this on their own without any help. They could create social media handles or a blog to get the word out, spin up a group on meetup.com, find sponsors, create a talk to present and then invite their friends to come. This requires a lot of personal investment, and while some people will be successful in doing this all on their own, others will not.

You can be supportive without being prescriptive by setting up a program that includes a directory where they can list their group, a small budget so they can get reimbursed for refreshments and snacks, a guide that helps them plan their meetings, sample content that they can present, and access to speakers from your company and the community. They can still choose their own content and run their meetings how they want, but you have significantly reduced the effort it takes to run a successful meetup, and this will result in more groups, meeting more frequently, and with better agendas.

Another benefit from not controlling the process is that the community members inspire each other. Nowhere has this been more apparent than in the rise of dozens of Salesforce community-led conferences around the world. The very first Salesforce community-led event was in 2011 when Midwest Dreamin' was held in Louisville, Kentucky with 100 people. By 2018, Midwest Dreamin' had 750+ attendees, but even more importantly it has inspired over two dozen community-led events around the world, from Down Under Dreaming in Melbourne Australia, to Punta Dreamin' in Punta Del Este Uruguay to London's Calling in London England, to Jaipur Dev Fest in Jaipur India.

Jaipur Dev Fest itself inspired a wave of events in India including Hyderabad Dreamin and India Dreamin'. While we've had a hands-off approach to these events to allow them to grow on their own, we've built a web directory to help promote the events and created a standardized way to offer Salesforce speakers and sponsorships so that we can contribute in an equitable fashion across all the events. But the events are theirs, and they have the freedom to find any other speakers and sponsors they wish - and to follow any format.

So what are some of the ways that we pave this path for our community?

- Carefully craft messaging that outlines the values we hope our community will uphold

- Make resources freely available including documentation, code, presentations - we've even created a free "workshop in a box" called BAM (Be A Multiplier) so community members can run their own workshops

- Create online directories to help promote meetup groups and community-led events

- Give access to Salesforce speakers - while ensuring that we don't dominate their events

- Shine a light on developers in our community who have created impactful programs or resources, to inspire others to follow their path

- Give feedback and advice around content, activities, and experts without being prescriptive to avoid diminishing creativity

Once you've paved a path and raised awareness of the amazing things people are doing in your community, you will be amazed at how inspiring this is not just internally but externally as well.

Grow champions

When you give people room to follow their passions, they can find amazing solutions to problems you didn't even know you had. When it comes to helping your community feel empowered, you need to do three things:

- Make them feel like insiders & part of your family

- Give them the resources they need to succeed

- Highlight & amplify their success.

At Salesforce, we use the Hawaiian word 'ohana to describe both our employees and our community. In Hawaiian culture, 'ohana represents the idea that your family members are tightly connected with each other and responsible for one another, whether related by blood or by choice. There are many ways to make your community leaders, and aspiring leaders, feel like part of your family, from hosting regular calls where you can interact, inviting them to meet your product managers and engineers and including them in focus groups or getting their feedback on your programs. To be insiders, your community leaders need to understand your products, your roadmap (as much as you can share) and even understand why you are making the choices you are making. Show that you genuinely care about their success in all your interactions with them.

Some of these champions will do amazing things completely unprompted, while others may strive for recognition as leaders in the community. Either way, creating a formal way to recognize these champions helps to celebrate their accomplishments and inspire others to follow in their footsteps.

Identifying and inspiring your champions

How do you identify your potential insiders? They are the people that stand out, for example, they can be your developer group leaders, bloggers in your community, people that have taken the initiative to create tools or other open source projects in support of your products, active participants in your developer forums or social channels, vocal advocates at your big accounts or consulting partners, or frequent speakers at your events.

You may consider putting together a special program for your insiders. At Sun we had the Java Champions program, at Salesforce we call them MVPs - a term that originated in the world of sports and originally stood for "most valuable player." By creating this program, it makes it easier to work with these insiders on a more formal basis. From regular calls to private email lists or discussion groups, to doing special summits at events or even dedicated events, by recognizing these insiders in a special way, you can inspire others to follow their footsteps or even come up with their own ways to contribute to the community. To make sure it's a fair process, we share examples of how community members have become MVPs in the past, guiding principles that determine eligibility, as well as details on the nomination process - which is entirely community driven. We also have an index with all 200+ MVPs so it's easy to see who they are, visit their community profile pages, and get in touch with them via social channels.

And these MVPs (or future MVPs) can do amazing things for your community. One of the coolest community-driven initiatives that has developed in the last couple of years is #SalesforceSaturdays. Started by Stephanie Herrera, a Salesforce MVP based in Austin, Texas, #SalesforceSaturdays bring people together on Saturdays to learn together. Whether your workday is too busy to prioritize learning, or you are looking to switch careers, sometimes the only time you can find to learn is your own personal time. And doing it together can help you progress further and faster than on your own. The #SalesforceSaturday initiative was initially an in-person gathering, but it quickly became a global phenomenon with people connecting with each other through the hashtag - and interestingly has taken off in India more strongly than anywhere else in the world, perhaps because developer groups typically meet on the weekends there.

Last year, there was even a global competition to see which Salesforce developer groups could earn the most badges on Trailhead. Reflecting the strong culture of learning and self-improvement in India, two groups ended up in a list of the top 5 community groups (New Delhi, Atlanta, Pune, Austin and Tokyo). As with many community-led initiatives, we didn't create it. We didn't approve it. But we did our best to amplify all efforts and shine a spotlight on the originators for their achievements. Shining a light on initiatives like these, and the community members who created them, is a great way to inspire future leaders in your community.

Sharing with your champions

Once you have identified your insiders, whether it's through a formal or informal program, you can start to do a lot more with them. We regularly get their feedback on our products, our developer program, and on our messaging for events like Dreamforce and TrailheaDX - and we truly listen to what they have to say.

Live discussions are always best to create discussion and a real-time feedback loop. As a product manager at Sun, I would regularly brief our Java Champions through conference calls in advance of any product launch and get feedback on messaging as well as roadmap input. When I was leading a redesign of the Salesforce Developer Forums in 2013, I worked with a handful of members of our community to get early feedback from them on wireframes and designs - a process which resulted in very insightful feedback that shaped our development process for the better!

It's generally a best practice to make as many of your resources publicly available as possible - ideally without gating them. This not only makes it easier for your customers to freely access your resources, but it also aids the growth of your community. Developers evaluating your technology don't have to go through an account team to learn about your products, consulting firms can skill up to help your clients with custom implementations, and students or job-switchers can consider making your technology part of their career path.

When it comes to making developers feel like insiders, you may want to go even further and expose information that you might think of as confidential, for example, early access to your new releases, roadmap plans, and even the opportunity to participate in roadmap development. At this point, you need to decide for yourself what you are comfortable sharing but it is perfectly reasonable to ask a subset of your community, those you think of as insiders, to sign the same non-disclosure agreement you might put in place with your customers so that you can feel comfortable sharing non-public information with them. This can serve to make them feel even more like they are part of your team - because they are!

Measure your success

The value of community can be hard to put a finger on. Implicitly, some companies understand that a strong community of developers helps drive customer success and adoption of your products. Other companies may be looking for a more direct connection to the bottom line. Certainly tying it to traditional business metrics can be a challenge, depending on the nature of your business.

I tend to think about the contribution of community in two fundamental ways: awareness & adoption and there are ways to look at the contribution of your community for both of these.

When it comes to awareness, I've put together marketing operation systems that have looked at how different resources and channels have contributed to deals, whether its new signups that originated from StackExchange, Reddit, Twitter, or Facebook or even referrals where developers tell their friends to check out our product(s).

Adoption can be trickier; how do you know if a blog post that one of your MVPs wrote helped your developers figure out how to use your latest feature? Sometimes, the best way is to simply ask your community what is helping them. To get this data, we do focus groups AND surveys on a quarterly basis, since this can be an excellent way to understand the value of different community resources. While asking people directly can have flaws (people don't always remember how they first discovered you or what was most helpful throughout their journey) looking at this data in aggregate across your community can give you a pretty solid indicator of what is working.

Once you figure out which tactics have value, align on these with your executive stakeholders so everyone is on the same page and then measure them, fanatically. Do it daily if you can automate it, or at least weekly if not. And then communicate your success. At Salesforce, we use our Chatter product to share our progress with our stakeholders on a monthly basis - we track the numbers more frequently for our own team, but do readouts every month to avoid information fatigue.

Some of the community metrics we look at:

- Total number of community members & monthly growth
- Total developer groups, new groups added, and meetings per month
- Visits to our developer center & number of Trailhead badges earned
- Number of community events per year
- Number of social media followers & monthly engagement (likes, retweets, etc)
- NPS Score from quarterly surveys.

But sometimes success is less of a metric and more of an emotional story. At Salesforce, we are fortunate that our products have genuinely changed the lives of many of our developers. From being able to get a career as a developer without having the benefit of a formal technical education to switching to Salesforce from a technology that is less fun to work with or has fewer job opportunities, to using the Salesforce product to change the course of their company. By telling these stories about developers in our community, we are also able to highlight the human successes that come out of our community each and every day.

In conclusion

While this may read like a plan you can follow to build your community, the reality is that the community builds itself. Your role is to help it grow and shape its path with the programs you put in place to bring people together and champion your leaders, the successes you choose to spotlight, and with the way you treat the developers that make up your community.

At Salesforce, we are fortunate to have an incredible community that has grown around our platform. Our community truly feels like part of our family, they give back to others in an incredible way, and in many cases have even built their careers around our products.

While every community is different, one thing that is common across every community that I've been privileged enough to work with, whether it was the Linux community, Java, Ruby on Rails, PHP, or Salesforce, is that the people that make up your developer community are your greatest assets.

Chapter 4 | Repositioning Your Brand To Developers

Siddhartha Agarwal: Group Vice President, Product Management and Strategy - Oracle.

This chapter describes what Oracle has been doing to reach a new generation of developers. Our goal was to change the perception of our company in the eyes of software developers outside our traditional customer base, those who think of Oracle as an enterprise mission-critical software company, but not one that can help them build modern cloud native applications. We wanted to raise awareness of our cloud platform for building microservices, and container/serverless applications, our support of open-source projects, and our innovation in areas such as chatbots, artificial intelligence and blockchain. Our goal was for these developers to see Oracle's Cloud Platform as a rich canvas no matter what languages, databases, or tools they wanted to apply.

Our strategy included building a personal connection with developers via a series of intimate developer events around the world (branded Oracle Code). We have found that offering many, relatively small opportunities for engagement, and bringing content and connections to where the developers are working, affords us an effective way to engage and learn along the way. We also created a new online web portal focussed on developer needs, created lots of content to provide continuous developer education, built an external champions community, and launched an innovative program for engaging developers at startups .

Introduction

If there is a general theme throughout this book, it is that the cloud era has changed the nature of software development, and developers face the twin challenges of creating new, cloud-native applications, and migrating existing applications to the cloud.

Developer organizations inside companies often go through their own evolution of cloud adoption. Among the first uses for the cloud is development and testing (dev/test) environments, which developers can license, provision, and use instantly without the bureaucracy, delays, or capital costs required for going through the IT department.

From there, developers use cloud resources for building more sophisticated applications, and experiment with new technologies, tapping into free trials, pay-as-you-go services, and vibrant idea-sharing communities, including lots of code sample sharing.

Once new applications are written for the cloud, companies often find it easy to bring those applications into production simply by expanding and scaling up those cloud resources, adding testing and security, and integrating those new cloud-native applications into their existing IT infrastructure.

Reaching a new generation of developers

Since its founding, Oracle has nurtured and supported Oracle database, Java and developer tools communities, via Oracle-led technical online forums, and community lead online and offline engagement. There are also a range of initiatives around Java, which Oracle acquired along with Sun Microsystems in 2010, culminating in the annual, multi-day JavaOne event.

We realized that we needed to encourage developers to experience Oracle Cloud - especially those who had never worked with Oracle beyond using Java or Oracle Database. We needed a new approach to reach out directly to developers who are building cloud native API-first applications, and who are embracing containers, AI, and serverless computing.

The success of Oracle's cloud platform and infrastructure depends on these developers. The technologies they choose in development are the ones that de facto become the production environments on which their businesses are built. Oracle wanted to win the minds, and then the hearts, of these developers.

As one of the largest software companies, we may have no shortage of name recognition as a database, Java, and middleware company. However, in this cloud native era, our goal is to connect with developers who weren't already using Oracle products. We knew Oracle's traditional means of marketing, branding, and customer engagement would not work on these modern developers, who don't often respond to messaging that emphasizes ROI and discusses market share.

So the initiatives we pursued were all based on this understanding: developers are not like other individuals involved in product specification, evaluation, and purchasing. They must be engaged-with directly, with a free flow of information in both directions, and with opportunities to try the products.

Who we are

I lead the Global Developer Initiative for Oracle, in addition to Product Management and Strategy for the cloud platform, with responsibility for defining and executing strategy and revenue growth across cloud services for application development, mobile computing, chatbots, Internet of Things (IoT), API management, and integration. My team serves as the key leadership interface between engineering, sales, and marketing, and is responsible for driving Oracle's global developer engagement and ongoing relations. In my experience, a small core team of individuals are best equipped to define the direction of ongoing developer engagement, and to make rapid decisions to ensure that the engagements are successful. I put together a team of just five core cross-functional leaders to drive the developer marketing effort.

In past roles, including a previous stint with Oracle in the early 1990s, I've worked as a developer, founded companies as CTO/VP Engineering, and run sales and field operations in managed services, security, and application server companies. I know from experience the defining role developers play in deciding the fate of technologies - and technology companies.

The rest of this chapter will describe how we approached developer marketing through online and in-person engagements, and the lessons we learned in doing so.

Strategy for developer engagement

We knew very early on that successful engagement with modern developers required the following:

- Significant online content
- In-person engagements
- Quality free education
- An external champions community
- A program to engage developers at startups.

Ongoing online engagement

We created a lot of online content to demonstrate the value of cloud-native application development. We launched developer.oracle.com, a website designed to let developers jump right into the technology areas most of interest to them - from databases to chatbots - and get practical content including peer-written articles, hands-on labs and workshops, videos from sessions on the Oracle Code tour, code samples, and GitHub links.

The developer.oracle.com site is meant to reflect developer interests and trends, not replicate or replace Oracle product specification and documentation pages. Each technology page on developer.oracle.com is run by an Oracle developer community manager, who keeps the page fresh with the latest content and ideas from Oracle sources, product managers, and from around the web.

In addition, developer.oracle.com also has become a deep well of developer-focused video content, a lot of which sprung naturally from the Oracle Code event tour. By videotaping many Code sessions, Oracle created a steady stream of fresh thinking from experts around the world that developers could access online.

We also aggregated all the various Oracle blog sites targeted at developers, into a single Oracle Developers Blog, to allow Oracle technologists to communicate directly with the developer community about the latest trends and products.

Our community managers interviewed experts on site at Oracle Code events (which we explain later), streaming them live via Twitter and recording them for replay from developer.oracle.com. We also held three Code Online events in 2018 that drew inspiration from the live events, including the inclusion of non-Oracle speakers, who brought real-world use cases and peer-to-peer credibility to the attendees.

We also started sending out a monthly developer newsletter to stay in touch with the community on an ongoing basis. Like developer.oracle.com, the Developer newsletter focuses not on product pitches, but instead on the issues and news developers care about, and it includes practical, actionable links to resources like workshops, and code samples, blogs and how-to videos.

Here are the lessons we learned about online marketing to developers, in some cases, through our own trial-and-error, and in other cases, from observing best practices from other software companies:

- Put everything online. Developers could be working at 2pm or 2am, and when they want something, they want it now. For example, you can't take a day to provision downloads of demonstration or trial software. If that developer is working at 2am, he or she wants to try something now.

- Provide rich, constantly refreshed educational content, including articles, code samples, videos, how-to's, and structured classes, and make it easy to download them. Nothing says "cool" like having classes taught by experts in the field on the latest technology. Nothing says "old-school" like highlighting yesterday's buzzwords.

- Make it easy to find a community of like-minded developers with forums for questions and discussions. The whole industry has seen that the success of communities like Stack Overflow shows the best, most trusted experts are the developer's peers who have solved the exact same problem.

- Newsletters can add value, but only if they are true newsletters with technical content and links to new material. Faux newsletters that are nothing more than marketing pitches will not only fail, but can also backfire and leave a bad impression. We're careful to make sure that our outreach to developer includes how-to's, code, more code, and even more code.

- Embrace developers outside your ecosystem, and invite them inside the tent to provide feedback in exchange for early access to technology and events. Many of them, if impressed with your offerings, will help evangelize your brand and share their credibility with their fans and followers. It was new for us to put local developers on-stage at our Code roadshow events; at most Oracle events, the stage is dominated by Oracle executive and partners. While many developers are introverts and would never go on stage, others enjoy the limelight, and find it rewarding (and beneficial for their reputations) to present in front of their peers.

Continuous developer education

Oracle has always offered educational opportunities for its customers, and developers are no exception; we provide beginner, intermediate, and advanced-level courses that can be taken online. It's essential to allow developers to learn at their own pace, whether it's snacking on a quick lesson, or sitting down to attend a series of formal classes, with their employer's backing. We created a wide array of educational programs including:

- Non-product-oriented MOOCs (Massive Open Online Classes), which are taught on both fundamental and cutting-edge topics. Right off the bat, we offered MOOCs for free; we saw from other industry offerings that trying to turn MOOCs into a money-making business would be a turn-off for developers. Our goal isn't to make money from developers directly, and we don't want any barriers to learning from our experts. Rather, we want to embrace anyone who want to enroll in a MOOC, which takes a real commitment, since a typical MOOC runs over a period of weeks, and requires a 4-6 hour commitment to review videos and take quizzes. Adding to the incentives, certificates are given for those who pass the quizzes. For some attendees, those certificates may have value at their current or future employer.

- Product learning. We brand many of our product-oriented training and education sessions 'Oracle University'. Many of our Oracle University sessions are on developer topics, and with emphasis on the cloud, we're continuously expanding our new offerings with developer training on our cloud services. Oracle University classes can lead students to professional certification, which can be essential for career growth, and perhaps, lead to more trials of Oracle products by developers and their employers.

- Free trials and usage credits are powerful tools for developers - far better than webcasts or scripted demos - so they can try offerings in their own time, and on their own projects, either at home or at work. We are continually removing the friction that it takes for developers to sign up for online accounts and try software; we have learned that developers aren't patient with red tape or bureaucracy.

Engaging with startups

Another step in the educational direction are customer startup accelerators. Providing resources to developers working at startups can be essential for their success, and, in-turn, provides precious product feedback from cutting-edge users. For example, if anything is unclear with an API or its documentation, or if an API needs additional functionality, we want to learn about it sooner rather than later. Developers working in startups tend to push the envelope on using cloud services, and are not shy about providing feedback and new-feature requests.

Such programs are expensive to create and operate, but can lead to deep and lasting relationships with creative, growing companies. Oracle currently offers two accelerator programs, which are unusual in the industry in that our company does not take an equity stake:

- Oracle Startup Cloud Accelerator is a residential program enabling early to later-stage startups with a hands-on and immersive six month program. It includes co-working space, credits for technology services, mentoring, and - perhaps most important for these nascent companies - access to some of Oracle's enterprise customers, and its global partner network and investors. Our accelerator is sited in nine cities around the world, from Austin to Bangalore to Sao Paulo.

- Oracle Scaleup Ecosystem is a nonresidential, virtual-style program designed for mature startups and venture capital and private equity portfolio companies to enable rapid growth and scale. This is a newer program for Oracle.

External champions community

It's critical to engage external communities to communicate with developers on your behalf. This provides access to new audiences, and leverages the authority and credibility of partners. For example, in 2017 we launched the Developer Champion advocacy program, to complement the existing Java Champion program. Developer Champions are not Oracle employees, and are, for example, contributing to our open source projects, or are authors on contemporary development approaches, or speakers at prominent Oracle and top industry conferences. Developer Champions (like our Java Champions) enjoy a close relationship with Oracle, and often evangelize our initiatives to the broader developer community and ecosystem.

Oracle code events

Oracle put live events at the center of the developer engagement initiative so that developers could build a personal relationship with each other and with Oracle, and us with them. We created a new global program of dozens of intimate developer events, called Oracle Code, around the world, to augment our large annual JavaOne developer conference in San Francisco. Offering many small opportunities for engagement - and meeting developers where they are - afforded the most effective, and affordable, way to engage. And it provided for rapid changes and iterative learning that let these events continuously improve as they progressed. The events have been essential for bringing together local developer communities, letting them share ideas, and giving them a place to get hands-on with Oracle technology. Thus was born Oracle Code: a series of free-to-attend, one-day events that would traverse the world, with 35 events popping up in 31 different cities in 17 months, from Buenos Aires to Bengaluru, from Chicago to Shenzhen to Paris.

The Code Events were unlike anything we had produced before. The team deliberately chose to create relatively small events, for us, with only 300 to 500 attendees at each.

One guiding principle of the Code events is that they would not be all about Oracle. The event team published a call-for-speakers for each and every Code event, giving local experts (and even our competitors) a chance to speak to their peers about their work. Many speakers shared insight on open source projects they're working on, showing how these innovations could be applied to enterprise development. That call-for-speakers meant there was no cookie-cutter agenda for these events. Instead, the sessions were shaped by the interests and expertise of the local development communities.

The Code events traveled the world from March 2017 through July 2018, passing through cities in Asia, Europe, North America, South America, and the Middle East. While each event was relatively small, with only a few hundred in-person attendees, the reach was huge, both from the live events and from the web, through streaming during the event and on-demand video afterwards. Overall, Oracle Code notched up more than 600,000 developer registrations, from more than 31 countries.

A related initiative is what we call Oracle Code @ Customer, where we create and produce Oracle Code events for specific customer accounts, as well as to top ISV partners and global systems integrators. These provide access to different developers, many of whom have not had previous contact with Oracle. Our goal is to ensure that the Oracle Code @ Customer events are as engaging, exciting, and effective as our broader road-trip events.

In some cases, the Code @ Customer events were requested by the customers (through their Oracle representatives) because they had a large number of developers who wanted to be trained, or because they had specific technology topics that needed to be addressed, such as specific competitive technology they were migrating away from, and embracing Oracle. We were happy to satisfy those requests! In the case of integrators, this allowed them to host or co-host developer events for their biggest customers (or prospects), and also allowed them to highlight their own capabilities, product lines, and service offerings. These proved to be very popular, and we believe successfully positioned both the integrator and Oracle as innovators in cloud development.

There were several ways that the one day Oracle Code events were different than traditional multi-day Oracle conferences - and all these changes were designed to fit developers' interests, improve the on-site experience, and provide diverse viewpoints and technical insights. We knew that developers don't want a heavy-handed marketing pitch. We wanted them to hear many voices, and we wanted to receive their input and hear their stories too.

There were 200+ speakers rotating through all the Code events in 2017 and 2018, and many were developers from local companies. This provided a local flavor and air of authenticity that a pure Oracle-based speaker roster couldn't deliver. For another, there was a tremendous emphasis on hands-on workshops, going far beyond what Oracle had tried in the past.

Knowing that developers often learn best by playing, the Oracle Code events offered ways to combine tech learning with tech fun. At some Code events, developers could take a coding challenge in game form of an adventure in deep space, complete with Star Wars-style lightsaber sound effects. Completing the mission - which involves shooting down an enemy spaceship, hacking into the enemy's database, and identifying the coordinates of the evil empire's reactor core - required using languages including Java, Python, PHP, and JavaScript.

The affinity of many developers for brewed beverages is legendary, and so the Code Events provided several fun ways to engage with delicious libations - from coffee to beer - while experiencing practical applications of cloud computing. We presented it as follows:

Got a few minutes to try the IoT Cloud Brewed Beer from a local microbrewery? Extend manufacturing processes and logistics operations quickly using data from connected devices. Tech behind the brew: IoT Production Monitoring, IoT Asset Monitoring, Big Data, Event Hub, Oracle JET.

Robots Rule with Cloud Chatbot Robot: Ask NAO the robot to do Tai Chi or ask "who brewed the beers"? So how does NAO do what it does? It uses the Intelligent Bot API on Oracle Mobile

Cloud Service to understand your command and responds back by speaking back to you.

What we learned about events

In planning Oracle Code, the events team needed to rethink a lot about the look-and-feel and type of events the company runs - which were quite different than our huge annual Oracle OpenWorld conference, or for our smaller events focused on executives or senior managers in vertical industries. From attending developer meetups and other conferences designed for developers, we knew that developer events should look different than buttoned-up C-level conferences, which affected not only the topics presented, but the nature of the speakers, and even the timing of the event, and its agenda.

The events team had to present a unified view across lots of cloud services to developers. It had to reassess the type and format in which we produced technical content, the type of people to recruit to our Developer Champion advocacy program, the user experience within our cloud trials, and the nurturing programs we used once developers engaged with us.

This also required changing the mindset of sales and field marketing teams, to not just invest in programs that generated immediate pipeline. This required explaining that realizing the benefits of developer-focused programs requires patience; it's unlikely to pay off in deals closed this quarter, or even next quarter, for developers who have never engaged with the company before.

After all, developers are not prospects. They are certainly influencers, and in some cases, they may have formal or informal sign-off on platform adoption. However, metaphorically speaking, you don't take developers out for a round of golf, and try to close the deal on the 18th hole. Instead, you give them knowledge, you give them tools, you give them trials, and you let them work with your products at their own pace, on their own projects, at their own time. Developers don't want slick marketing collateral; they want code that works.

They want to be their own judges of whether you're a market leader or a tech innovator, thank you very much. They don't care about analyst reports; they care what their peers are thinking and saying.

In addition, unlike many prospects, developers aren't contacting us because they are in a buying mode. (Many don't even have purchasing authority for enterprise software like ours.) Instead, the developers attended our in-person and online events because they were curious. Curious about meeting Oracle people, about learning about a giant company, about cutting-edge tech like AI and blockchain, about cloud services that might advance their business or career. They came to learn, not to buy - and not to be aggressively marketed at.

Once up-and-running, the pace of production for the Oracle Code events was grueling - in some stretches events came once per week, often many time zones removed from the previous event location. Fortunately, Oracle's management committed the resources, both at corporate and at the local level, to assist with marketing, promotion, logistics, and recruiting local sponsors and presenters.

Essential to successful software development are frequent project meetings and code reviews, and the team took that same practice to heart for Code events. There was a full debriefing, debugging, and learning review after each one to fine-tune the events, such as assessing which sessions really resonated with developers, which were 'meh', and which fell flat. There were some of each, and to roughly summarize: Developers don't like anything that's vague or fluffy. They want to see the product, not hear about it. They want to see the code and touch the code. They want to see the actual running platform, not screen shots in a slide deck. And they don't want to hear from anyone who isn't technical.

Oracle also continually refined how to reach developers who weren't already part of Oracle's developer ecosystem, and how those developers best wanted to engage with Oracle before, during, and after the event. We paid rigorous attention to detail in order to understand the broad content concerns, and also the small details that matter in building close connections. For example:

- Developers work late and don't want to be dragged out of bed for an 8 am keynote. While sessions at Oracle OpenWorld and other major tech-industry events often start that early, we saw that wouldn't work for this audience. The kickoff talks at the initial sessions were sparsely attended, despite great speakers, as attendees straggled into the venue. We now begin the first presentation at 9 am, with much better results.

- On a personal level, I had to change. Initially, my appearance fit the corporate habitat I'm often in: sport coat, button-down shirt. I immediately realized this was not the best fit for this audience. But the t-shirt-and-jeans look wouldn't have been authentic for me either. After several iterations, I settled on slacks and a nice zip-up sweatshirt.

Each of the Oracle Code events turned out to have its own characteristics, and provided unique opportunities for the Oracle team to learn about the local developer community. For example:

- At the Austin event, we had a lot of excitement from the entire region's development community. Several attendees woke up early in the morning to make the 160 mile drive from Houston in order to attend the keynotes - and drove back the same day. Austin was one of the most engaged audiences of the first year. We saw engagement and enthusiasm very different than events located in the usual huge tech hub cities. It demonstrated why a road show model is great to build and connect with the developer community.

- Some things only work in specific locations or countries. At the recommendation of the local Oracle team, we often tried some experiences that sounded a bit odd at first to the people at headquarters - but really worked. One example of this came in India, where we set up a "selfie booth" where we had some of our advocates and speakers engage in technical discussions and take photos with attendees. It was amazingly popular - with a full queue all day even when technical sessions were running.

- Local events are a great way to discover hidden talent in your organization. Some of the local sales consultants who helped staff the demos turned out to be highly skilled and passionate about our products, and crafted ingenious new ways to connect with developers. One example came from a London staffer who helped us on the Internet-controlled CNC Router demonstration in 2017. The demo showed how to use a computer numerical control cutting machine to manipulate building materials. The employee went on to create some cool attendee demos that were showcased in San Francisco at Oracle OpenWorld later that year.

Some additional lessons we learned from the Code Events include:

- Smaller global events can be more successful than huge mega-events, because they allow for more engagement with diverse audiences who might not travel to the mega-event especially those who aren't already customers but might be willing to spend a day kicking the tires.

- The logistics for a road trip can be significantly more complex than for a single annual developer conference. Even the process of choosing dates for visiting cities world-wide can be a challenge, avoid local holidays and other big events in those cities - and tying them together into a single trip that doesn't destroy your staff. It helps to have a local presence in the geographies considered for the events who can arrange venues, find well-respected local speakers, figure out what will be fun activities, and highlight local preferences.

- Some developers are serious and all-business. Others learn through coding contests and games. Some are extroverts who will engage with speakers; others will never look up from their laptops. Be prepared for all types of attendees.

- Keep the price low. "Free" is a good price. Many developers lack budgets for attending paid events, or for travel outside their city. One-day events also minimize time out of the office so are attractive to employers and employees alike.

- Pay attention to details: Good food, good coffee, plenty of cold drinks and snacks. Have a party, if that fits your style.

- Bring in many voices, going beyond your own experts. Have perhaps one-third to one-half the speakers be from your own company, the rest from local experts and partners.

- Leave the sales pitches at home. That's not what developers want to hear. Beyond a short introduction, developers don't want to hear from your sales or marketing staff. Keynotes should be from techies, not from marketers.

- Have a casual style. Developers wear jeans and T-shirts, not suits. Also decide how much you want to tailor the developer experience to the local market, compared to, say, having a uniform, American-style look-and-feel.

- Be authentic and honest. Developers have a keen sense about when they are being patronized, or if flaws in products or technology are covered up. To win their hearts and minds, be candid with them.

- Provide free access to demos or trials. Again, although they are vital influencers, developers don't have large budgets themselves. Particularly if they are not already your company's customers, do everything possible to give them access to the product - before, during, and after the live event.

Oracle is now considering the next moves for developer engagement events. With all the lessons of Oracle Code in hand, we're ready for the large-scale, multi-day developer event we initially held off on.

Overall learning and best practices

Developers are essential to the growth and long-term success of Oracle's cloud platform and infrastructure service business, and we will continue to broaden and deepen our engagement with this critical audience.

By putting the developer in charge, offering excellent content and treating developers according to their preferences, we have found a way to help developers discover our company's technology, the side that's relevant to their goals.

One final best practice: Relentlessly listen to developers both inside and outside the ecosystem, and inside and outside the company itself, to get the best view on your evolving audience. What developers want is constantly changing. And thus, engagement must always grow and evolve to meet developers' needs.

- Understand that developers don't like to be sold to, and need to be engaged, not pitched. Anything that's purely a marketing effort will fail.

- Get executive buy-in and support for developer engagement, from the highest level.

- Define a small core team (handful or less) that defines direction, incorporates input, and makes fast decisions, and most of all, isn't afraid to make changes in mid-stream.

- Engage online and in person. The key is back-and-forth engagement and continuous education - not presenting one-way marketing messages.

- Think big, and execute in small increments showing some value in each increment.

- A lot of small activities can be more effective for reaching diverse audiences, as well as allowing for rapid changes and iterative learning.

- And always remember to be authentic, open, and honest in your developer engagement.

Chapter 5 | Connecting Developers With Experts

Thomas Grassl: Vice President, Developer and Community Relations - SAP

When software developers using your platform or tools need answers or advice, you might think that your company would be able to provide the perfect resources for them. And you would be partially correct. While developers do seek guidance from their vendors, they often prefer to get information from their peers; meaning from your community, particularly from external developer experts within it.

Serving up expert access from your company's workforce alone won't be sufficient. You'll need to encourage a network that provides expert advice from external sources. In this chapter, we discuss the key elements of an expert developer program and describe how to attract evangelists, product managers, and other highly skilled and motivated developers to provide their expertise to the broader developer community. We will discuss how to find experts, how to position them within the community and how to reward them.

Introduction

Founded in 1972 by five developers, SAP is now a leading provider of business software. Initially focussed upon on-premise solutions that covered everything from customer relationship management to enterprise resource planning, we have expanded into the cloud and technology space.

Whether installed locally, or enabled via the cloud, our solutions depend on the developers who implement, maintain, integrate and extend SAP software. Providing those developers with an expert network is essential. They need to be able to connect, to ask questions, to share information, and to give and seek feedback from SAP, and also each other. This information exchange explains why nearly 3 million developers visit our community every month to get the most from our solutions and their development efforts.

Fortunately for me, as the head of the company's developer and community relations organization, development is near and dear to my heart (pun fully intended).

I took on my role at SAP in 2012, but my expertise in development started long before that. I was a developer for years; I built development tools in C++ and worked with Java for Web Application development in the early days of the Internet. I still continue to develop to stay sharp.

In addition to development, I have covered other technical aspects, such as product management. I know how a developer works and thinks, which comes in handy when building and evolving the best possible channels for expert access.

Humility helps. As much as I know about development, I know there are experts who know more. Most developers recognize this truth, and while the very best may come to a community or expert group in hopes of spreading their knowledge (and building their reputations), they realize that these outlets can also teach them and make them more successful.

How to build a network of experts

Your network should be a good mix of internal and external developer experts, ranging from specialists to generalists, who act as educators and role models. They are positive representatives for your company and brand, but they aren't just cheerleaders. They're professionals who can teach and influence developers who are using your software. Moreover, they're professionals whom the developers will actively seek out for input and collaboration. Providing access to these experts will be seen as a valuable service to community members. It's also valuable to the company providing the community, as members can provide real-time feedback about the company's products in terms of what works and what doesn't.

At first blush, building a group of experts and a community for developers may seem like a classic Catch-22. A community without experts cannot succeed, but a community cannot succeed, and draw experts, unless it already boasts experts in the first place. In reality though, all facets are equally important and must be executed in tandem. It's not a matter of build it and they will come. You must build something that gives a reason for developer experts to come. And participate. And stay. And return.

A vibrant community depends upon both attraction and interaction. It depends upon a diverse group of experts for that reason.

Finding experts within your company

Typically, your network of internal company experts splits into two categories:

One group will consist of **Developer Evangelists** who are most likely to sit directly within your developer relations team. They are often (if not always) developers themselves, and they possess first-hand experience with the broad range of solutions that outside developers use. Given their direct experience with diverse solutions, these evangelists can speak knowledgeably to developers about a variety of technical topics.

The second group comprises **Product Experts**. They are more specialized, yet still gifted at relating to developers. Internally, they are your product managers and product engineers. Their contributions come from their deep know-how in their product areas; offering up information and insights to developers who focus on their products.

Internally, it is easy to spot some prospects for your expert network because you'll know the rock stars in your product and developer relations departments. Peers speak highly of them. I'm talking about product managers and evangelists who show initiative and speak at internal company and department events, as well as at external conferences, sessions, gatherings, and other get-togethers that developers frequent. Many are active in social media, and you'll see them tweet (and get retweeted) about relevant subject matters - a good sign of a potential candidate who will act as a company expert publicly. They may already be participating in other types of communities or writing for relevant sites. For example, if you visit StackOverflow, you may see them answering and asking questions about the solutions your community covers. A pro tip: generally speaking, you should check StackOverflow regularly. Monitoring other communities and sites is a must for spotting experts and even for getting ideas for improving your own community.

Other potential developer experts within your company may not be as visible, or may need nurturing. A call for experts is a good place to start. Post and make announcements within your company. The people who reach out to you might not have the chops yet, but by contacting you, they have demonstrated drive and enthusiasm. You certainly won't need to worry so much about incentives. The motivation for many internal experts is a desire to further their careers. Getting their names out and being seen are great motivators for anyone seeking advancement. You can entice them further by providing support for them to engage with external customers and developers in focus groups. Invite them to speak at events and pay for their travel. This support goes a long way - both literally and figuratively.

If you'd like to give your internal experts additional status, consider putting together a formal group that employees can strive for. At SAP, we're launching SAP Technology Ambassadors. An offshoot of SAP Mentors (a group of external experts, explained in more detail in the next section), this initiative is limited to employees who can serve as true ambassadors: the crème de la crème who are the best company representatives and speakers for developer topics.

Whether new recruits or veterans, your internal experts will need coaching and training so they are consistent in their presentation. For example, you'll want to encourage them to be visible contributors within the community, and you'll want to prepare them to meet the expectations that you set. Start simple with a list of responsibilities and a code of conduct so the experts know what they should do (investing a certain number of hours per week answering questions about their topics for example) and how they should do it (appropriate behavior). Your internal experts can make great presenters for hands-on trainings and labs on the products they cover. In return, they get to interact with the external customers and learn more about them, their needs and their priorities.

A developer program builds your external network

Finding developer experts outside the company may be a little trickier, but you'll apply criteria similar to those applied to building your internal network. You'll spot external experts speaking at events, participating in other communities, and generally establishing themselves as professionals who are knowledgeable about your technology. External experts will typically fall into the specialized areas that are either related to your company's products, or to a specific domain. That's because experts tend to specialize themselves. Even those familiar with a variety of software experience will tend to feel most comfortable with a core set of solutions.

Your job is getting the attention of the external experts you spot and giving them a reason to share their expertise.

This is where your developer program comes into play. A program for evangelists, product managers, and other highly skilled and motivated developers - like a broader developer community - is a method for providing expert access. But whereas the community is open to all types of members (developers primarily, but certainly not limited to that audience), the developer program is, not surprisingly, geared to the developer audience.

To break things down even further, our developer program concentrates heavily on three areas: awareness, engagement, and adoption.

Awareness, as the name implies, makes developers aware of products. Engagement educates developers more deeply about these offerings. Adoption includes tools and content that developers require to build and implement solutions.

Some members of the developer program may specialize in one area - for example, evangelists are great at engagement, but the experts often straddle all areas. Take our SAP Mentors initiative, launched in 2007. The mentors are the best and the brightest developers from outside our company. They provide a valuable service by guiding other developers and offering feedback to SAP, and they're capable of addressing each phase of the developer program's progress (i.e., awareness, engagement, and adoption). More specifically, they collaborate with SAP on topics ranging from products and features to go-to-market efforts, general strategy, and partnering. In exchange for their participation, they receive access to SAP events, invitations to meetings about special topics, recognition in the community and at conferences, access to our executives, and swag (such as individualized SAP Mentors shirts).

We've capped the SAP Mentors at roughly one hundred participants, all of whom are highly recognized experts in their fields. Naturally, a developer program requires far more than that, so while you can use initiatives to highlight certain experts, you'll want an extensive network of outside professionals.

To encourage external experts to join your developer program, you should have a strong online presence, for example on social media. Use it to make a positive impression and highlight your community and your developer program. For example, in the online community, look for new members who have written their first blog post or have taken a stab at answering questions. Encourage them. Give them positive reinforcement. You could promote their post through your social channels and within the community itself.

Offline, you can find experts at events, introduce yourself, tell them a bit about your program, and explain why their expertise could be a boon to it. A little flattery never hurts.

As with your internal group, you can't expect to survive with one crop of outside experts. Even as you're bringing in experts, you should be prepping the next generation. An established name isn't a prerequisite for program participation. To be sure, it's beneficial if your target audience recognizes your experts, but don't be short-sighted. You want to be on the lookout for future talent too. Remember: No expert - even popular ones - started as an expert.

The developer community

Your developer community combines everything from online destinations to in-person activities. The former includes your own community site, but also extends to StackOverflow, LinkedIn, and any other site where your audience can share information.

For SAP, in-person activities include SAP Inside Track events (where developers can network and learn) and local, informal meetups. We also support an activity called CodeJam, upon request from developers. We host these CodeJam events and provide an expert who can work with attendees to solve problems or work on coding together for a product.

A developer community provides a perfect channel for two-way communication with developers (who are also customers). Most developers seek communities where their peer members are not only company employees. They do, however, appreciate information from your internal experts, so I'm not suggesting that you exclude your employees from the community. Just make sure that they understand what your members expect, which shouldn't be a problem for your product managers and evangelists, who handle developer relations on a daily basis anyway.

Both a community and a developer program need focus, and focus comes from defining what they are. This may seem somewhat contradictory to what I noted earlier - emphasizing the need for a group of experts who cover a wide range of topics. But even a diverse group of experts requires a firm strategy for the program that gathers them together.

The importance of planning becomes evident when you connect the experts and the community. As you define the community, you'll find that you'll be defining the parameters for your experts as well. Your developer experts and community must complement each other. That's impossible if you define your community as a destination that provides areas of knowledge which don't match the talents and skills of your experts. This disparity would be disastrous.

With this in mind, consider how your experts should cover the complete range, from product specialists to evangelists with a broader base of knowledge. Your community should be equally comprehensive, but without getting too generic. Calling it a community for developers is a fairly broad statement. Does that mean developers can wander in and post about whatever they want, where they want? That invites chaos.

To help maintain order, we have established rules of engagement and moderation guidelines for our community site. On top of that, our seasoned members may kindly call out simple questions from new visitors (ones the rookies might have been able to answer themselves via a basic search). Having a community that polices itself can cut down the noise, but you also need to appreciate the fine line between strict enforcement and lax policies. It's not always easy, and we continually look for the right approach that welcomes all members while also maintaining quality content.

We also maintain order through the structure of the site itself, which gives direction. Think of the community in terms of the areas of a developer's expertise. (This shouldn't be too hard, considering you're doing essentially the same thing for the experts in your developer program!) These areas could range from products to wider topics to industries to specific functionality. When developers join a community, they will be joining for different reasons. It's important to think out these reasons and map them to the topics that interest developers,- which, as you probably guessed, should also be fairly close to the topics that the experts in your developer program cover.

In a way, the term "community" is actually an umbrella for smaller groups who are devoted to one or some of the topics within the community, not to the entire community itself. We discovered the layout logic of this strategy early on by building spaces that served as sub-communities, an approach that eventually evolved into tagging content and topic areas.

I should add, however, that we have revisited the tagging concept, because tagging is not always conducive to the tribal feeling of a dedicated space. The advantage of tags is that it flattens the site in a way which simplifies navigation. The downside is the lack of centralized sections for topics where like-minded developers can connect and enjoy a one-stop location that aggregates all content related to their specific area of interest - not just tagged content such as blog posts, but also relevant tips, a list of experts who can provide additional guidance, a breakdown of all topic-specific news, and so on. In short, visitors need a section for each topic that makes information more accessible and easily consumable.

Defining the community isn't simply determining which topics belong in it, though. The topics are part of what the community is (a destination for information about x, y, z, etc.), but the definition also needs to cover what the community does, or more appropriately, what members do in it. If you think of the community as a grouping of forums, then each forum should offer an identical experience. Typically, this experience amounts to sections where people can ask questions, provide answers, blog, collaborate, make connections, and so on. Ideally, your product managers and outside experts should monitor the sections corresponding to their areas of specialization, while evangelists can keep an eye on the bigger picture, chiming in to discuss general development trends and similarly broad topics that might cross multiple products and industries.

As an aside, even if you limit your company's contributions to the community, you still gain a major benefit, as community Q&A can lower the burden on your support department.

With all of that in mind, you could define the developer community as a place where members can get and share information about the topics you've identified as most relevant to your audience, and that can be supported by your developer experts. However, information is another broad term. What information precisely?

A company must understand what the community needs, and what it wants from its experts. It's tempting to turn the community into a marketing tool to churn out company-generated messages. To some degree, this will be unavoidable. For example, your colleagues may want to to post something promoting one of their upcoming webinars, an action that qualifies as marketing, and members will accept this content, as long as the webinar covers a topic of interest to them. But if the webinar strays from the area of interest, their comments will be less than kind.

The trick, then, is finding a balance, which is one of the many things we learned when we launched our community nearly 15 years ago as SAP Developer Network, which evolved into SAP Community Network and is now known simply as SAP Community.

And what of the content itself? As I noted above, a community can give a company an outlet for promoting their events and product release details that developers need to know. But most developers come to the community because they're stuck and they need questions answered quickly. Active members - the experts you want to draw and keep, and eventually introduce into your developer program - will keep an eye out for questions and jump in to answer. They may also blog about their areas of expertise, sharing knowledge that may answer questions before a developer even asks.

But why would the experts have an incentive to do any of that? They could be paying it forward by helping to educate developers in a way that they themselves were once educated. They might be doing it for their careers. Someone who is a recognized expert, especially a consultant, becomes a desirable service supplier. They might be doing it for the rewards (some of which I mentioned earlier, many of which I'll explain in more detail shortly).

And they might even do it to learn more themselves. Many experts will tell you that, when answering a complicated question or writing a blog post, they will research the topic more deeply and thereby expand their own expertise.

That should give you a sense of how to define the community: what it should cover, what it should provide, and how it should operate. It should also help you understand the motivations of why people participate. But I've not yet shed light on how you establish the community, so that developers will see it as a go-to destination for information and guidance, and so that experts will feel inclined to participate actively.

As I noted near the beginning of this chapter, these activities do not, nor should they, follow a set sequence, where step A gets you to B, B gets you to step C, and so on. Everything should happen in parallel. Even as you're laying the groundwork for a community: building out areas where members can ask and answer questions, publish blog posts, and collaborate and socialize; your internal experts should be involved and serving members. At the same time, you should be looking within and outside your company to bring in more traffic: increasing the number of developers using your resources when they are in need of answers and increasing the number of experts capable of providing the answers. Some cynics might dismiss this philosophy as attempting to build a plane while you're also trying to fly it. I would counter that no community is ever truly complete, and the actions required to build and maintain it are ongoing efforts. If you ever think your community is finished, then it is indeed finished: but not in the way you intended!

Rewards and recognition

Once you have an established base of developer experts and a mechanism for finding new ones for your program, then what? Make sure that your program gives the experts a sense of identity and purpose.

Your experts add up to a major component for your online community, but always remember that a community extends far beyond the online world. Community is everything, from informal get-togethers to formal events. You should encourage these, promote them, host them, and make participants feel welcome. If budget allows, help fund the events or offset costs so your experts can attend yours.

SAP TechEd is our biggest annual event for developers, in fact we host three SAP TechEd conferences each year in the autumn: one in the United States, one in India, and one in Europe. They provide our program with an excellent opportunity to give expert access on a global scale, and our product teams are particularly active in these intense sessions, bringing their knowledge directly to the attendees.

During SAP TechEd, we roll out the red carpet for our developer program members, the SAP Mentors. They have their own space on the show floor, they have their own special events, the SAP Mentors get free tickets to the event, they are given special speaking opportunities, and they even get front-row seats at the event's keynote. We make every effort we can to thank our experts and show appreciation for their efforts. Our Developer Heroes and Community Heroes place the names of exceptional contributors front and center, by introducing who they are and what they do and why that's important.

However, if we limited expert participation to SAP TechEd, we'd be missing out on a big chunk of the year. That's why we have other events: our internal experts hold SAP CodeJam events where they conduct hands-on sessions with developers. Our external experts hold SAP Inside Tracks (SITs) to give developers a deeper dive into topics. In all cases, the experts often conduct these sessions locally. Since SAP is a company with offices around the globe our internal and external experts come from many different countries. We truly do share our expertise around the world.

To handle these events successfully, your experts will require effective public speaking and teaching skills. The shy ones might limit themselves to the online community, but wherever possible, you'll want experts who can operate both online and in person. If they're comfortable standing in front of a room of developers, they'll likely be comfortable on camera as well. So if you have a YouTube channel, use it to interview your experts and promote the videos. You need to invest in support since it must look professional. At big events, we have a studio and we invite them in to discuss a topic, but alternatively, it can be a roving reporter at the event or an online interview, such as recording a video chat. Let them shine and show off their expertise. They'll appreciate the opportunity and you'll promote your community as a destination where visitors can benefit from the interviewees' expertise. The videos also provide yet another way to access experts. Our SAP CodeTalk series of interviews in our SAP Community channel on YouTube could give you some food for thought for shooting your own videos.

We also make sure to salute the community's efforts. For example, our popular Member of the Month feature shines a spotlight on up and coming community participants, to show our appreciation and encourage them to get more involved. We also have a system of badges and points that we have implemented in a gamification system which allows members to build their reputations.

Motivations for community participation are similar to motivations for participating in a program for experts. In both cases, the experts are volunteering to share, but they also understand that they'll be reaping benefits as well. It's no surprise then that a program for developer experts and a developer community fit together so nicely.

Lessons learned

I've established what goes into offering access to developer experts, but you're probably wondering where things can go awry. Beware hubris and deaf ears. Your program gathers experts with the expectation that developers will listen to them. You should listen to these experts as well!

In many ways, the experts know what developers need because they're developers themselves. You can provide the tools and support, such as the formal program and the various aspects of the developer community, but don't ever assume you have all the answers. Be willing to learn from your experts when they come to you with ideas to improve the community, the developer program, and so on. That doesn't mean you'll change and implement everything they ask for. But you must keep the channels of communication open so they can comment about the program and the community experience itself. If they don't think you're taking them seriously, they'll stop taking you seriously. And they'll drift away. Considering that you want developers to mimic the experts' behavior, you don't want your program participants to leave!

We learned from this mistake with our developer program and community. We're still learning. After introducing changes to the program that our most vocal experts didn't accept, we had to step back and re-evaluate. At the same time, we decided to overhaul aspects of our developer program to bring in new perspectives while giving our long-timers a chance to continue to contribute as alumni. This is important. You must scrutinize your program and community constantly, so that you don't fall behind future trends.

Looking forward

Speaking of future trends, you will likely have noticed that my advice about finding and nurturing experts, building community, etc, requires a lot of legwork. In the future, this work doesn't need to be so manual and nor should it be. AI and algorithms already exist to connect the dots for like-minded people - bringing together groups of people with similar tastes or pointing these people to things that might interest them (based on previous behavior). The same logic can be applied to experts and communities. With the right automated tools, you can more easily identify experts in specific fields and connect people more quickly to the content that might apply best to them.

Regardless of the approach: whether you set up tools to find experts or rely on good old-fashioned investigation or some combination of these, one thing is certain. Your developer program requires a solid base of experts and a bullpen of up-and-comers. You must find them, coach them, keep them. Your developer program and community, and all of your attempts to provide expert access, cannot succeed without them. So look for the experts within your company and outside of it, and never stop searching.

Chapter 6 | Hands-On Labs For Effective Developer Relations

Larry McDonough: Director, Product Management - VMware
Joe Silvagi: Director, Customer Success - VMWare

Throughout its journey, VMware has maintained a very strong relationship with IT Admins, in much the same capacity as traditional platform companies maintain an ecosystem of application developers.

But, as the ancient Greek philosopher Heraclitus once said, "change is the only constant in life". IT Admins change. Developers change. Oddly enough, their roles over the last few years have started to overlap. Developers are increasingly taking control of the infrastructure upon which their apps are built, tested, and deployed. Likewise, IT administrators are increasingly turning to scripting and coding the infrastructure they manage.

Technology is contributing to this convergence: agile software development methodologies have led to continuous integration and continuous deployment and the "DevOps" process. Other contributors include technologies like containers, Docker, Kubernetes, Serverless/Function as a Service (FaaS), microservices, and service mesh.

In this chapter, we will describe the VMWare Hands-on Labs, which are virtual computing environments that grew out of the need to bring up a trial of VMware's product stack rapidly. While the Hands-on Labs originated as a means to help existing and potential customers experience and learn about VMWare's products, they have expanded and brought value to the company in many ways that we didn't originally expect.

Introduction

VMware was formed in 1998 and is best known as a virtualization and cloud computing company. The company pioneered the virtualization of the x86 architecture which led to a major disruption in the IT industry. With VMware's platform, customers can run and manage their corporate workloads in virtual machines which run on fewer real computers, cutting capital expenses, maintenance costs, staffing, and even electricity bills. Over the years, our company has expanded its virtualized compute infrastructure to include virtualized storage (vSAN) and more recently, virtualized networking (NSX).

Our company has had a shifting relationship with developers. VMware's very first product, VMware Workstation, was indeed targeted at traditional developers, giving them a way to build and test applications destined for multiple operating systems on a single machine. Later, the company's core products were primarily for IT Admins but, after a number of acquisitions, VMware developed a Platform-as-a-Service (PaaS) business based on an open source project called Cloud Foundry which supported application deployment and lifecycle management. When VMware spun this business out in 2013, setting its sights back on the Infrastructure-as-a-Service (IaaS) layer, one could imagine that there wouldn't be much need for developer marketing anymore.

However, that has certainly not been the case and, in fact, the number of different developer segment has increased over time. The confluence of IT-admins-that-code and developers-that-manage-infrastructure converge has renewed our focus on developer marketing. As traditional roles evolve and infrastructure technologies become more complex, one thing has become apparent: developers are becoming increasingly influential in deciding which IT technologies their companies use. This raised a fundamental question for our company: how do we make a complex and extensive technology platform - like a software defined data center - accessible and easy to learn? In the rest of this chapter, we will discuss the Hands-on Labs technologies, which provide an answer to this question, and much more.

What are Hands-on Labs?

Our Hands-on Labs are virtual computing environments running in the cloud, paired with some training. They help developers and IT Admins get our complex VMWare platform up and running in minutes, acting as a technology showcase and allowing users to explore it easily and effectively.

Hands-on Labs are one of the main attractions at VMworld US and Europe, but are also available online, with over 1,500 Hands-on Labs taken per day, adding up to over 1.5 million taken since 2013. An estimated 900K Hands-on Labs will be taken in 2018 alone, a 59% increase over 2017. There are over 400,000 active users around the globe. Each Hands-on Lab has on average 11 Virtual Machines, and users average 51 minutes per session.

The platform is perhaps one of the biggest drivers at our VMworld conferences, where admins and developers take the Hands-on Labs in preparation for their certification exams. Hands-on Labs have also helped to increase the effectiveness of our beta and early access programs, and we use a similar, but slightly different, labs platform to educate our global support organization enabling them to replicate customer environments. We've even built a robust and profitable education business upon Hands-on Labs. They have evolved from showcase to a tool for education, and even sales.

Throughout the rest of this chapter, we'll review some of the uses for Hands-on Labs and explore each of the ways they have benefited our marketing and outreach efforts. And lastly, we're not done finding ways to use Hands-on Labs to drive innovation and add value to our ecosystem. We'll take a peek at a new developer engagement framework that VMware has been rolling out and how Hands-on Labs play a role there too.

Enabling hardware certification testing and early access programs

Like operating system software, hypervisors and virtualization software require tight integration and testing with thousands of technology partners including OS vendors, SoC suppliers, GPU providers, storage solutions, networking and security hardware and software. The complexity and necessity of certification testing for all these hardware and software products is intensive.

With software cycles getting shorter and faster, we had to find ways to get our products into the hands of our customers without waiting for certifications across thousands of different hardware types and configurations, which can take a lot of time. VMWare uses Hands-on Labs to help customers experience and test early-access and beta versions of our products. For example, vSphere 6.0 was made available for a selected number of customers (in the hundreds) who wanted to test it and provide feedback more than 6 months prior to its release. The long lead time allowed the customers to determine if their hardware or software was going to work early on, with plenty of time for them to make changes in time for release. It also gave us time to fix critical bugs.

The Hands-on Labs offered customers an environment that looked like a complete datacenter with all the software and hardware they would expect to see. It came loaded with VMware's latest products so the customer could try out all the functions, explore the new features and, yes, find and report issues which we had missed. VMWare engineers and product managers could access a specific Hands-on Lab and view the problem issue first hand. We could debug the product and apply a fix quickly and efficiently. This included serious bugs, as well as minor issues that had work-arounds. This enabled us to release the product without having a fully tested and bulletproof upgrade and installation solution, since it all took place behind the scenes via the Hands-on Labs.

Using Hands-on Labs for early access and beta programs provided such tremendous value that we continued to expand the products we'd test and the number of customers we included. In the end, the biggest benefit of this program could be measured by the results. The number of issues reported from early access via the Hands-on Labs, by a few hundred customers, turned out to be equal to the number of issues reported later by the thousands of customers who used the standard release beta binaries.

Field engineering

The initial intent of Hands-on Labs was to introduce new products, allowing customers to see and touch the new technology. There was one particular product at VMware that pushed the Hands-on Labs into the next level.

VMware's Network Virtualization product, NSX, had no way to download a trial and required certain physical network settings. The Hands-on Labs were the only place to try the product. As the popularity of NSX grew, not only did the VMware field engineering teams need training, but customers also became interested in this training. While real networking hardware was not easy to come by, we could easily spin up and spin down our vPods (virtual contained labs) from a Hands-on Lab to provide training to the customers.

We would give each trainee a vPod to use for the duration of the course. If they broke it, they simply logged off and spun up a new one. They could work through the manuals that were developed as part of Hands-on Lab training or go off course and do their own thing. The Hands-on Labs provided a full functional environment that allowed them to do that. They could experiment, try out functions, all without worry of having to rebuild it if they broke the system. It was as simple as logging off and back in again. In a complex virtual environment with lots of applications running, it's often a lot easier to start over, than it is to figure out exactly what broke and then work out how to fix it.

We discovered that if the customer did not initially have the hardware or time to dedicate to a full scale proof of concept, the Hands-on Labs provided an alternative way to investigate the technology to the point they could see the value in scaling up to a trial. In some cases, we kept the vPods around for days, versus hours, to allow the customer to dig deeper into the technology.

Driving VMWare's education business

VMware's education team originally provided traditional instructor-led classroom training, typically offered as a 5-day course. While classroom instruction has many benefits to customers, such as direct access to the instructor, and the networking benefits of meeting other professionals, it also has drawbacks, such as getting travel approved, rearranging schedules, and spending time away from family.

When we decided to additionally offer the courses online using self-paced Hands-on Labs, we weren't sure how customers would react. Since there isn't a live instructor, should the cost of the class be the same? However, because the instructional content was essentially the same, we decided to launch the service with the same price as the instructor-led course. We decided that customers would appreciate the savings they made by not having to travel, and the extra time they were able to spend with online Hands-on Labs. Ultimately, customers found the pricing model to be highly acceptable.

Since the training was self-paced and could be taken whenever, and as often as, the customer wanted, the only question we had to answer was what should be the duration of the Hands-on Lab? As we were providing access to real hardware and software infrastructure, we couldn't leave those resources tied up indefinitely.

We considered 30 days as an option, but when we launched the first online Hands-on Labs, we wanted to be more generous, so we settled on 45-day duration. We got no pushback on this from customers. In fact, they loved the extra time they had to run through the training, and they really liked the freedom of fitting it into their schedule. But, when we looked at the data, we found that most people were waiting until the back half of their 45-day window to complete the lab. They really didn't need that much time.

We now have two options for course duration - one is 30 days at a higher price point mainly targeting enterprise customers and the other is 20 days targeting SMB/individuals customers. We did some experimentation at 15 days at the SMB/individual price point, but after some analysis, we identified the optimal time to keep a lab active was 20 days. Any less than this stressed out the customer, and any more than this meant we were paying for lab resources that weren't being used. If a customer requested an extension, we granted it. In addition, we also introduced a subscription model where a customer buys a number of user seats for a year. The "users" can then take as many classes (available within our portfolio) as they want within that 365 days duration. The subscription is also available at different price points for different customer segments.

A problem we encountered early on as we converted the instructor-led content to an online format, was that some of the content wasn't well suited for Hands-on Lab format. We had to redesign the courseware for a Software-as-a-Service (SaaS) framework that allows students to keep moving through the content. Hands-on components could be assignment-driven, but other components of the instructor-led courseware had to be reworked, like video-content and demonstrations, simulations, and basic instructional content.

Our content development team within Education Services made all the content updates. The team has instructional designers and learning experts who consult with instructors, take student feedback, and analyze usage data to design courses. They are constantly improving the design. At the time of launch, our objective was to test the market with a modest investment in content change, and once we were convinced of the commercial feasibility, we made more investment in infrastructure and design to scale.

Once we reworked the content, growth and the success of the online labs skyrocketed. Within 2 years, the online Hands-on Labs were generating more than $10M in revenue. Although our online classes are growing at a faster rate than our in-person classes year over year, the in-person classes remain our largest segment in actual numbers. We also optimized their cost by modularizing them and making them more infrastructure-efficient, automatically putting them to sleep to preserve resources when they're not being used and reconstituting them as needed.

We have also provided an alternative, hybrid-approach, for those that want it. Students of the instructor-led classes have the option to purchase a discounted Hands-on Lab version of their course. This allows them the ability to run through the content again once they get home in their own time. We're always looking for new ways to improve the education experience and are considering new features like Hands-on Labs "office hours" where students can ask questions to an instructor over chat.

Best practices

When building a lab of this nature, keep it open and off any type of rails if possible. This allows the lab and the effort that went into building it to be of multiple uses including uses you may not have considered when it was initially built. The open nature of the environment is what made it so successful.

Promoting Hands-on Labs to the developer audience

To promote the Hands-on Labs we use our Twitter account (https://sdata.me/BpgPkl) and blog (https://sdata.me/pLIYzW) as part of our online and physical multi-channel strategy. The Hands-on Labs are a core element to every major marketing event both online and physical for VMware. We are also integrated in all of the core VMWare product pages as part of the evaluation experience.

Looking ahead: driving product innovation through Hands-on Labs

Today's developer is dealing with an ever-increasing list of complex, and often conflicting and overlapping technologies. Every year, there is more to master: new languages, development frameworks, coding methodologies and platform topologies, such as cloud-native, 12-factor app development, SaaS, service-mesh, AR, VR, IoT. There's a lot to learn. Developer research also shows us that developers are increasingly self-taught with different educational foundations, many without any formal computer science training.

So, how do today's developers find answers to the questions they seek? Where do they go? Some may go to Stack Overflow, but overwhelmingly, the developer's tool of choice is Google.

As a platform provider, it's imperative that we make sure the correct answers to common developer questions about our platform are found easily when they're Googled. This can be improved, not solved, through diligent search engine optimization (SEO). But, is this the best we can do? No.

Often, the search results developers receive are close, but not the best. Since software technology is changing very fast, and release cycles are very short - weekly is common, but some platforms update daily, or even hourly - Google results will prioritize the volume of hits for a particular search (popularity) over the recency (newness) of the search. Even as this improves, the real winner in this scenario is Google. Whether or not your developer finds the answers which they seek, Google finds out what your developers are looking for. We find this to be an undesirable side-effect of the "Google-is-your-best-developer-tool" mentality.

To improve the accuracy of the information our developers seek, and remove any non-contextually aware intermediary search engines, we've taken the approach of incorporating "Developer Centers" directly within our products. In order to achieve this, we started by building out all our developer resources as separate services, accessible through REST APIs and then bundling them together in a Developer Center module, making it easy for product teams to make them available in their products.

The first two tools we created in this framework were API Explorer, for browsing APIs, and Sample Exchange, an open index of VMware and community-contributed sample code. We've also cross referenced these services so they can be used in context. For instance, when a developer is browsing APIs, we have automatically linked and made accessible, any associated code samples that use those APIs. The same is true for documentation and SDKs. A great example of this can be found in a post on the "VMware {code}" blog, titled "Enabling Developers in VMware Cloud on AWS", found at https://sdata.me/VnhNnC.

Now that we have this Developer Center framework in place and it's starting to show up in our products, we're exploring how to incorporate Hands-on Labs as a developer service to augment API Explorer, code samples, SDKs, etc. We believe that developers benefit from having a working environment with all resources available to them where they can explore and try out APIs from within a pre-configured "Hello World" app. As with the other developer services, the Hands-on Labs service will be contextually linked to the other services as well. We're still exploring the best way to do this.

Ultimately, the purpose of all our developer outreach efforts, is to make it easy for developers to quickly build and innovate on our platform, and we believe Hands-on Labs will continue to help us reach this goal.

The authors would like to thank Pablo Roesch, Andrew Hald, Nidhish Mittal, and Gordon O'Reilly for their contributions to this chapter.

Chapter 7 | Growing Up By Scaling Down: How A Small Developer Event Can Make Big Impacts On Your Ecosystem

Luke Kilpatrick: Senior Developer Programs Manager - Atlassian
Neil Mansilla: Head of Developer Experience - Atlassian

At Atlassian, we take a multi-pronged approach to supporting our developer ecosystem, including methods that you're already familiar with, such as holding a general developers' conference, hosting an online hackathon, providing a dedicated online developer community forum, etc. In this chapter, you'll learn about another, unique approach we use to take developer engagement to a new level: an event program called App Week. We have found the program yields phenomenal results, including new apps and vendors launching on the Atlassian Marketplace, improved developer relations and a strong product/platform feedback loop, plus a healthier ecosystem overall, in spite of its compact size. While this program may not be a exact fit for the needs and stage of your business, we believe you'll come away with applicable tips for improving the outcomes of your developer events.

Introduction

"Having an open platform makes not a successful platform business, nor thousands of tinkering developers a healthy ecosystem."

Over the last decade, you can find countless examples of companies that opened up their APIs to the public in the hopes of sparking innovation and creating business value, but never realized those aspirations, and ultimately ended by shutting them down. However, a handful of companies have managed to succeed with their open platform approach. While there are numerous factors that separate the successes from the failures, a very noticeable difference is in how the successful companies understand, cultivate, and invest in their developer ecosystems. Developer events such as Apple's WWDC, Google I/O, Salesforce TrailheaDX, and Twilio Signal are key examples of how companies are making significant investments in this area.

At Atlassian, events have also proven to be a critical part of cultivating an ecosystem, bringing together customers, developers, Marketplace vendors, solution partners, trainers, and more. In 2008, Atlassian held its first Atlas Camp developer conference. It was small and informal, comprising of around 80 people; these days, Atlas Camp attendance is capped at around 700 people. Atlassian's first customer conference, Atlassian Summit, was held in 2009, and had just a few hundred attendees, but more recently, it hosted around 5,000 attendees.

As Atlassian's ecosystem continued to grow, it needed to find a way to continue building a healthy developer ecosystem, remaining personal and responsive. Atlassian has committed to doing this by running a new series of developer events (in addition to Atlas Camp), and this chapter describes the thinking behind the strategy, the lessons learned, and recommended best practices from the company's Developer Experience (DevX) team. The team provides support for, and advocates on behalf of, all developers in the ecosystem and supports Atlassian's developer events, from helping to organize content and tracks to providing onsite developer support.

Note that this chapter is not about how to run developer events on a large scale, but rather, how and why to focus on the qualitative aspects of an effective developer event and how it benefits the health of the ecosystem.

Why do you need an ecosystem?

At Atlassian, the tone of our relationship with developers ("open by default") was set by the co-founders from very early on. From the start, customers were given access to our source code, allowing them to customize and extend the functionality of our software to their needs. After all, being open and sharing information are part of our company's core values. Between 2002, when the company started, and 2012, when we launched Marketplace, thousands of developers were building custom apps and integrations for Jira and Confluence. From our core company value of being open, an ecosystem was born.

We build tools for teams of all sizes - from startups to enterprises. Because our customer base is so broad, building features and solutions for every specific niche is impossible. One of the purposes of having an ecosystem is that it frees product development teams from having to develop features that address every niche use case.

A good product works hard to be an 80% solution. In other words, your main product should solve 80% of the customers' problem. The remaining 20% is where huge differentiation comes into play, and where an ecosystem can get your product to be the 100% solution for your customers. Your ecosystem may have experts in respective fields that can help to extend and custom-fit your product to the special needs of your customers.

Why do you need in-person events?

Hosting and attending in-person events can be quite expensive in terms of both time and money. With all of the advancements in online communications, including virtual meetings, webinars, and real-time chat, why do we still do them? Online tools can't quite top meeting people in real life, face-to-face, for making a personal connections, building empathy, and learning from one another. All of these are key factors for nurturing a balanced, healthy ecosystem.

Physically meeting someone establishes a personal connection that goes beyond the code, and beyond the business aspects. It engenders empathy - the ability to understand and share feelings of another. If this feels all too personal and squishy - good, you're on the right track. Understanding the motivations, challenges, and tribulations of the developers in your ecosystem can help your company make better informed decisions, and vice versa.

As Atlas Camp grew into a larger developer conference, we felt that the scale was great for making announcements about new features, and for many attendees to learn about them, but it also became more difficult for people to build connections. While only a fraction of the size of WWDC or Google I/O, the depth of the connections, conversations, and learnings at Atlas Camp became increasingly diluted.

Learning with our developers has been a key part of how we've managed to grow and build trust in our ecosystem. Learnings between developers in the ecosystem through in-depth conversations have also played an important role in the maturation of our ecosystem. The Atlassian Ecosystem team felt an alternative, more intimate event was needed to create the opportunity for more two-way dialogue and meaningful human interactions. The solution we came up with was adding a new series of smaller-sized events called App Week.

What is Atlassian App Week?

App Week at its core is a focused work week, where Atlassian developers, product managers and business people from across our company come together with the developers, product managers and business people of our third party vendor community. App Weeks have the goal of helping our ecosystem developers to create new apps (or improve existing ones) based around a theme supporting Atlassian's business goals. The event is purposely kept small and invite only, with a maximum of around 120 developers and 30-40 Atlassian staff to support them, a very low attendee:staff ratio. This ratio provides an accelerated path to success for our attendees as often the person you need to talk to the most about an API or feature is right there, ready to help.

Any ecosystem vendor can apply to attend an App Week. Details about an upcoming event are posted in our online developer community forums, newsletter, and blog. Vendors are selected to attend based on the theme and goals of the event. Staffing is also based on the same criteria.

App Week is different from a general developer conference in more ways than just being smaller in size. There are no content tracks - just a handful of short talks that are salient to the week's goal and theme delivered by Atlassian product managers and engineering leads, and in some cases third-party ecosystem developers. There are no sponsor booths with marketing collateral. The vast majority of the time is for engineers to work together to solve problems, and for dedicated 1:1 meetings where decisions makers can discuss future plans and implementations.

The first App Week

The very first App Week (formerly named Connect Week) back in 2013 was held in Amsterdam, Netherlands, with a small group of about 40 people - 25 third-party developers and 15 Atlassian team members. This was held before the beta launch of Atlassian Connect, a framework for 3rd party developers to build apps for Atlassian Cloud products, including Jira, Confluence, and Bitbucket. A successful ecosystem of 3rd party developers was already established around our server-based (on premises) products, but the launch of our cloud products introduced a different app development and deployment model.

This first App Week was critical for the Atlassian development teams to learn which features the framework needed to allow developers to port their server-based apps over to cloud. Likewise, the third-party teams wanted to learn more about what Atlassian was doing before investing in the new cloud model.

The first event was a success in that it helped lay the groundwork for the Connect platform. But the conversion of these 3rd party server apps to cloud was just the start of a five-year long journey, which in the software world is almost a generation.

From the feedback gathered at the first App Week, and the subsequent feedback gathered during the beta period, Atlassian released version 1.0 of the Connect framework in March 2015.

The birth of the modern App Week

By late 2015, the Atlassian ecosystem team noticed a lack of high-quality, successful cloud apps in the Marketplace. A number of our top server app vendors told us about their problems developing on the cloud platform: the cloud framework and APIs didn't have all the features they needed, the addressable market of customers on cloud wasn't large enough, building and managing multi-tenant apps was difficult, etc.

The framework feedback was not easy to act upon, as the Atlassian product teams were laser-focused on meeting customer needs with new features and functionality, and not on the ecosystem. Unlike server app development, where the developer has broader and lower level access to resources and components, developers had to work with more restrictive sets of APIs and UI integration components when building apps for cloud.

As Atlassian product teams shifted their focus to the ecosystem and making Connect framework improvements, we decided it was time to host another App Week. More than two years after the first App Week, the second event also took place in Amsterdam, Netherlands, with over twice the number of people - 90 in total, including 60 third-party ecosystem attendees (developers and product managers from 30 different companies) and 30 Atlassian team members. Our goal was to port as many of our top performing server apps as possible over to the cloud, which meant helping 3rd party developers to work with newly shipped Connect framework components, as well having our Atlassian product teams learning what else the ecosystem needed to be successful on the cloud platform.

By the end of the week, over 30 cloud app demos were presented by vendors, including 5 of the most popular apps on the server platform. The week also resulted in new features being created for the Connect framework. Within a month of the event, the number of cloud apps in our ecosystem increased by a third, including some of our most popular server apps, which became available for the first time in the cloud.

The success of App Week had a great impact on our next Atlas Camp developer conference in Barcelona, Spain, held in May 2016. The outcomes were highlighted in the keynote, including the progress on the 3rd party cloud apps and the new features on the Connect platform. It was absolutely clear that the direction of the ecosystem was being influenced from the discussions, learnings, and work being done at our developer events.

Trust in the ecosystem was being earned, and the attendees gave this Atlas Camp its highest rating ever.

App Week had proven to be incredibly valuable for both our ecosystem vendors and for Atlassian, so we ending up holding two more in 2016 - one in San Diego, California (August), and another in Sydney, Australia (December). Both events also yielded great results, with more apps expanding from server to cloud. In 2017, we brought App Week back to Amsterdam, Netherlands (March) and then to Austin, Texas (July). With each App Week, we continued to iterate and improve the experience, incorporating feedback from the ecosystem.

Evolving App Week

The event held in Austin, Texas (July 2017) was the sixth App Week we held. At all six events, the focus was primarily on cloud app development - helping vendors port apps from server to cloud, and improving the Connect framework. For the next App Week, we applied the same formula, but set out to accomplish a different goal.

In addition to server and cloud versions of our software, we also offer Data Center editions, which is like our server version but with support for active clustering for high-availability, redundancy, and performance. Large enterprise customers were happy to find a plethora of Marketplace server apps designated as Data Center Compatible. However, some apps were not performing well, or in some cases failing in large scale clustered deployments. The decision was made to launch a program to verify Data Center app readiness, with new requirements for apps and vendors to meet before an app can be designated as compatible with Data Center products. While all of that seems logical, making changes in the Marketplace can also result in serious financial impacts for some ecosystem vendors.

In the spirit of our company value, "Don't #@!% the customer" (DFTC), the theme of our next App Week was Data Center - a departure from our cloud objectives from the last 6 events. The first goal of this event was to help ecosystem developers understand how to make their apps work well in a clustered environment, dealing with complexities like long running tasks, cluster locks, memory usage, etc. The second goal was to learn what the ecosystem needed from us, such as testing tools, clear program requirements, etc. The App Week in Amsterdam, Netherlands (November 2017) was not only interesting in that it focused on Data Center, and not cloud, but also because it was very similar to the first App Week - where the conversations, feedback, and learning were more important than the coding.

For the next App Week, we took another bold turn with a user experience and design theme. Held in Key Largo, Florida (March

2018), the event included not just engineers and PMs, but designers from the ecosystem vendors and Atlassian. The spirit of learning and sharing was in full force at this App Week, and several serial attendees expressed their surprise and delight at how much value their teams got out of it.

App Week has been truly evolving throughout the years. With each iteration, we've evaluated the outcomes, and incorporated both external and internal feedback to make the next event even more effective.

Lessons learned

Hackathons that work

Many companies have the idea of "let's just add a hackathon to our user conference and see what happens!". Without clear goals and a strategy, what usually happens is a train wreck that lasts 12 to 48 hours, with developers solely focused on putting together a fancy or funny demo to take home a glittery prize. Most hackathon projects die shortly after the event, or worse, never make it beyond the presentation deck.

App Week is definitely not positioned as a hackathon - there is no competitive element. In fact, it's commonplace to find vendors helping each other by sharing knowledge, soliciting and providing feedback, or sometimes even getting heads down with code or APIs. Focusing the event on collaboration and working together, as opposed to a competition, has brought a level of trust into the ecosystem and helped foster a real sense of community. Fostering trust and cooperation provides long term benefits to the ecosystem that's worth more than any hackathon prize.

Hackathons done correctly can create great results - but they need a specific time, theme and challenge to achieve success and ROI. Atlassian is famous for ShipIt, an intra-company hackathon held quarterly, where the goal is unbridled innovation and fun. There have been a number of really amazing things to come out of ShipIt - from internal apps, Marketplace apps, to even full-fledged products, like Jira Service Desk.

Atlassian also runs a public online hackathon called Codegeist with very specific goals of bringing new apps into the Marketplace. It's held once a year, and runs between 2 and 3 months in length. For an app to even be considered for judging, it must be live on the Marketplace, meaning that the app has to fully pass through the Marketplace app review process. Compared to traditional hackathons, where the results often range from demoware to falling short of a minimum viable product, Codegeist is aimed at delivering fully baked apps, ready to serve customers. Even if an app doesn't win the contest, the real prize for the developer is having an app on the Marketplace with an opportunity to reach Atlassian customers.

Codegeist has a proven track record of driving success in the ecosystem and Marketplace. For example, the first-place winner of Codegiest in 2007 was an app called Checklists for Confluence. The app was built by a single developer start-up called Comalatech. Today, Comalatech is a multi-million dollar business, with over 40 employees around the world, and over a dozen apps on the Marketplace that have been installed by more than 10,000 customers. Many other top-grossing Marketplace vendors got their start by participating in Codegiest, including Easy Agile and Code Barrel.

Fun developer events start with great instructions

Accurate, well-maintained technical documentation is a must for developers to start engaging with your platform at an event. Getting started should be simple, and onboarding should be measured in minutes, not hours or days. It is frustrating for developers to waste half of their time at an event struggling to get their bearings on the table stakes, such as getting an environment setup and working with API authentication. If your docs are less than perfect or your platform is a bit more complex, provide quick-start guides, or starter packs (sample apps that are easy to grok and then build upon) that help developers accelerate.

Avoid the echo chamber

Every ecosystem has its shining stars - the vendors that generate the most revenue, or seem to be making the biggest investments. While their attendance is important, events should not be focused solely on those top vendors. We believe that having between 20-40% "new blood" is important. Doing so not only helps new ecosystem developers to accelerate their development and business growth, but it also helps expose a more diverse set of ideas and problems to your product and engineering teams. Growth is important in any ecosystem, and with a good balance of experience at your event, the attendees also help each other grow.

In the fall of 2016, a solo developer named Tim Clipsham applied to attend an App Week event we were planning for Sydney in December. At the time, he had built an app for Confluence Cloud, which sold decently enough for him to start considering leaving his day job at a national bank, and focusing on running his company, Good Software Co. We invited Tim to attend because he was showing promise as a small Marketplace vendor, and he also happened to be Sydney-based. At the event, Tim was incredibly productive, putting together a marketing plan, working on a brand redesign, and starting the journey of porting his cloud-based analytics app for Confluence Server. Since attending App Week in 2016, Good Software was recognized as the "Best New Vendor of the Year" at Atlassian Summit 2017 in San Jose, California, and has added several new people to the team.

Get your staff away from their desks (and their daily work)

In an effort to save on costs, companies often opt to hold developer events at venues close to where most of the supporting staff are located, such as their own office. This sounds like a great idea, saving money on travel and venue, and having a huge pool of talent to draw from to help support the event and the ecosystem vendors. What's not to like?

In our experience, we found that holding an event at or near the office lowered the quality and character of App Week. For example, App Week in Sydney (December 2016) was held in our office, close to where the Atlassian engineering team is based. While this seemed like an ideal situation, the irony was that staffing the event proved to be very difficult. Even though hundreds of Atlassian engineers were a stone's throw away, peeling them away from their regular work responsibilities proved to be a challenge.

It's best to hold your event off site, or in an office that is not the home base for the majority of the team that is staffing the event. While it does introduce more costs, it helps to significantly improve the quality of the event. Staff members can focus on supporting the event and meeting the attending ecosystem developers, rather than being pulled back to their desk or into other meetings. Ecosystem developers, who are also making significant investments to attend, appreciate the attention and reciprocal dedication being shown by your company.

Another benefit to holding the event at a remote venue is personal networking and socializing within the ecosystem. If the event takes place close to where your team members live, most of them will just go home for the day, which results in a missed opportunity for people to connect after the day ends. At App Week, each day ends at 5pm sharp and is followed up with a scheduled happy hour nearby. With everyone away from home, we cluster together and connect as people, creating bonds, sharing stories, relaxing, and having fun. It's similar to being a freshman in college or away at summer camp - everyone is equally out of their element, and friendships are formed quickly. Holding your event at a single venue, with both hotel and event space, is ideal, but having folks stay at nearby hotels can also work. The key is socialization after the computers get put away.

Best practices

The App Week program has been incredibly successful and it works for Atlassian, but what best practices can we share for you to apply to your own developer events?

Skin in the game

Having your product development team buy in and commit to supporting the events, to the point that they're willing to invest a week of their time away from the office and day-to-day work, is of paramount importance. Having this support allows ecosystem developers to interface directly with product and engineering teams, who have the expertise to help them accelerate development. The other benefit is that it tightens up the feedback loop, helping your product team to better prioritize and manage their roadmap by having a sharper view on the value of requested features and the impact of bugs.

Set your theme

Next, establish a theme for the event. A theme helps set the tone for what the event is trying to accomplish. If you're asking for support from other internal teams, choosing a theme that aligns with their team or department goals is helpful. Themes also help your ecosystem vendors to justify their investment of attending your event. If a theme isn't well defined, then you're signaling to everyone that you're holding a general developer event. For example, the theme for the first few App Week events was "Build your server app for cloud." Later, we set themes that were more specific, such as "Data Center readiness" and "Experience design and performance."

Select your location

The next three things that matter for your event: location, location, location. Ideally, the event is held in a place that is convenient for your ecosystem developers to attend, taking into consideration their travel and lodging costs. Choosing a location that entices people to come is also helpful. It should come to no surprise that Amsterdam, San Diego, and Key Largo were very popular event locations. Lastly, try not to be drawn into holding your event at your office as a cost-saving measure. Do not underestimate the value of having your team members stick around, instead of driving home, so they are building connections with the ecosystem after the computers are put away.

Next, you need to source a venue that fits with your event. For App Week, we typically look for a minimum of 3 meeting rooms, but prefer 5 or more. The most important room to consider is the main meeting room, where you will hold your presentations, stand-ups, and demos. We have found both rounds and class room style layouts work best. Theater seating for demos is preferred, but the seating does not have to change. The other rooms provide a variety of work spaces away from the main room - quiet spaces where developers can code in peace, a restaurant-fashion setup room with multiple tables that seat a few people for small groups meetings, etc. If you can add extra rooms, a "boardroom" or small formal space is great for private group conversations, such as business and partnership development meetings. Lastly, if you're lucky with the weather, having outdoor space where people can work is also appreciated. Just be certain that the WiFi works out there!

Finding the right venue can be challenging. Create an RFP (request for proposal) with all of your event requirements. There are services that help craft RFPs and submit bids to event venues, like MeetingsBooker and Cvent. Many hotels in the US provide a free event space if you pay for a food and beverage minimum and a hotel room block. Based on booking patterns, we generally reserve a room block for about 40-50% of the attendees, and encourage everyone to book quickly for the best rates. We suggest negotiating flexibility with the hotel for expanding the block if there is demand.

Food for thought

For catering, morning coffee service is a requirement. If you have the budget, breakfast is also a nice touch, but optional. At App Week, having breakfast does help get most attendees downstairs and ready to go for the 9am start. Lunch, on the other hand, is essential. You don't want to disrupt the flow of the event with everyone hunting and gathering for food in the middle of the day. Also, mix it up, and ensure there's food variety between the days. It's important to ensure that you cater for different dietary requirements. As for dinner, this is something we do not recommend you provide. There too many factors to consider, including preferences, dietary restrictions, group logistics, and costs. But more importantly, dinner is the perfect time for the everyone to go out and connect with one another. Make sure to provide a list of recommended local restaurants.

A/V and WiFi

Another logistical consideration are your audio visual needs. For presenting, you'll need a projector, a screen, and a lectern to hold the presenter's laptop or notes. Make sure you have HDMI, Mini DisplayPort, and USB-C adapters on hand, which should cover most contemporary laptops. You can save hundreds of dollars per day by shipping your own company projector rather than renting one. We have found the most success with handheld microphones over clip-on lavalier style mics. We recommend having two mics, one with a stand for the speaker on stage, and one for passing around the audience for asking questions.

This applies to any developer event, but with App Week it is even more critical - you need to provide fast and reliable WiFi. We've found that it's best to secure minimum bandwidth of 100 Mbps downstream, 25 Mbps upstream, and a high-capacity DHCP address pool. You should estimate at least 3 IP addresses per attendee to account for their laptop, mobile phone, and additional networked device (tablet, smart watch, etc.) The ecosystem developers, as well as the staff, are getting work done - pulling down repos, pushing code, running tests, as well as streaming music and video conferencing. We've all been to events with awful WiFi - it's asinine. Do not overlook the importance of good WiFi, and don't implicitly trust the venue sales person - talk to the person who manages the routers and access points.

Creating your goals

Establishing goals for your event is absolutely critical. Having well-defined goals helps you to get buy-in from stakeholders and makes it easier to measure success. Only with these measures will you know how to improve your event, and justify future investments in the program.

Some common goals for developer events include: creating awareness, collecting product and platform feedback, driving adoption, building trust, training developers to use your APIs, helping developers to improve how they market to your customers, etc.

For App Week, our goals center around driving adoption, building trust, and collecting feedback, therefore we keep the event small and more personal. For goals centered on developer awareness and acquisition, sponsoring or speaking at larger developer conferences might be more appropriate (i.e. AWS re:Invent, Pycon, TechCrunch Disrupt, etc.) For goals that focus on developer training or marketing, a larger format, general developer conference, like Atlas Camp or Salesforce's TrailheaDX, might be better suited. Make sure your goals and event type match up.

Tailoring your event to your goals is key in choosing the format, staffing and location - so establish your theme and goals early, as they'll help guide you toward making the right decisions along the way.

Measuring your outcomes

Setting goals is key, as is how to measure your progress against them. At Atlassian, we've historically used Net Promoter Score (NPS) as well as a few other metrics to establish the quality of the event. For App Week, NPS can be problematic due to its smaller size. Just 1 or 2 individual detractors can cause severe negative swings of 5 or more points. Starting at the Key Largo App Week (March 2018), we shifted to a "top 5 metric" where attendees rate the event on a scale of 1 to 5 - one being "poor" and five being "awesome." This provides us with a percentage based result which we find better reflects the quality of the event compared to NPS, and addresses the susceptibility of those enormous score swings.

Every App Week concludes with a demo session on the last day where all teams get to show what they've built, and share what they've learned. Demo day serves as a tangible target and motivator for the teams throughout the week. For measuring the outcomes of the demos, we suggest having two to three staff members give each presentation a basic grade. When a vendor's demo really shines, our Ecosystem Marketing team follows up to explore ways to help showcase their new app or new features. It's also important to follow up with the vendors that did not do so well throughout the week, and investigate why. These cases require a follow up by someone in developer relations, with the goal of learning what went wrong, and what you can do to improve the next event.

At the end of the event (after the demos are complete), surveys are sent out via email - one survey for all of the ecosystem vendors that attended, and one for staff members that supported the event. The survey data helps us to understand how the attendees felt about the event - what they loved, what could have been done better, and what they actually worked on and accomplished. In our closing remarks, we kindly ask everyone to fill out the survey, and send follow-up email reminders up to 5 days after the event. Collecting this data is of utmost importance, so don't be shy about asking them them to fill out the survey.

Sharing with the company

After the event, it's great to share a recap with your company to highlight what was accomplished, what was learned, and provide recognition to your teammates for their support of the event. Doing so helps the different departments and teams within your company understand and connect with what's happening in the ecosystem, and the value that it brings. At Atlassian, this would be an internal blog post, because that's just part of our culture. In fact, it's typical to find multiple recap posts from individuals that attended. But it can take any format that your company uses - email, newsletter, town hall presentation, etc.

After every App Week, we receive feedback from ecosystem vendors stating how they were able to accomplish in a week what would normally have taken several months or longer; or sharing their gratification for Atlassian's support of the event. And while that's wonderful to hear, it's twice as rewarding to hear our internal product and engineering team members comment on what they learned from the ecosystem developers; or how those lessons have influenced and inspired them to help improve the platform, and support the ecosystem.

Summary

Intimate developer events, when planned and executed well, can drive value across multiple dimensions. In addition to helping drive business objectives, small events also promote relationship building, trust, empathy, and learning, which are all key to building a well-balanced and thriving ecosystem. Starting with clearly defined goals, choosing the right style and format, and getting buy-in and participation from all key stakeholders, is essential. Measuring your outcomes, applying what you've learned, and evolving your efforts will only push your ecosystem strategy flywheel faster.

Chapter 8 | How To Connect With Developers When You Can't Meet Them

Pablo Fraile: Director of Developer Ecosystems - Arm
Rex St. John: Senior IoT Ecosystem Manager - Arm

Imagine you are put in charge of marketing a successful, fast growing product to developers. However, your nearest competitor is about 20 times your size and, unlike them, your company doesn't make a physical product that developers interact directly with. Welcome to developer and ecosystem marketing at Arm, where our primary objective is to drive awareness, loyalty and adoption of key Arm features and technologies to create "Pull Through" for our newest products by reaching out to developers and introducing them to the latest Arm functionality.

Introduction

Our company designs and sells a series of flexible blueprints, libraries and tools, which it licenses to a vast network of ecosystem partners. These partners then use, deploy and manufacture physical implementations of our microprocessors based on our blueprints, doing so under their own brands to an audience of their own developers. For our team, this is the challenge: Arm's business model means that developers rarely interact with us directly.

Arm processors outnumber humans on earth by more than 10:1: our suite of microprocessor technologies can be found in billions of medical devices, satellites, robots, drones, cars, servers, laptops, tablets, wearables, digital personal assistants and nearly every mobile phone on earth. However, our company is relatively small in size for those typical to the semiconductor industry, with a headcount of approximately 6000 employees. We tend to operate behind the scenes despite wielding a large influence in our sector. So, while Arm's influence is on a scale similar to that of companies like Amazon, Microsoft, Tencent or Google, connecting with developers is a particularly tough challenge.

Our situation is not unique. Most companies don't have the intimate relationship with developers that the Internet giants enjoy, yet still need to find a connection to their ecosystem. In this chapter, I will describe how Arm has tackled this challenge, but first I will introduce myself, and then introduce Arm.

I come from a background in product management, business development and technology partnerships, and joined Arm in 2016 to build a stronger developer ecosystem presence for our mobile line of business. Perhaps because of my relative lack of experience in the field, I've spent much of my time studying how successful companies reach their developer audiences, and how those strategies could be adapted to Arm's particular position in the ecosystem. This chapter summarizes some patterns I've observed, with real examples, and in some cases, with real names too.

You may know Arm as the company behind the mobile and embedded processor architecture. That is one of our biggest claims to fame, but Arm also makes many other products, from graphics processing units (GPUs) to server processors, and huge volumes of software to enable those products in the market.

One of Arm's roles includes building or contributing to compilers, libraries, and tools across multiple verticals. In some established markets those tools are extended, packaged and distributed by the 'tier-1' developer program owners. Examples include Android in mobile, Unity in game creation, and Red Hat in server.

The audience we aim to serve are developers who work "close to the metal" on hardware, independently of verticals or platforms. For example Android developers writing native code, mobile game developers looking for the last ounce of performance, embedded firmware and IoT device makers. A platform developer program will typically provide the platform-specific tools, software and advice, but may not address hardware specific questions in any depth.

The main challenge for us is reaching the audience, and making it aware of Arm's contribution to their developer environment despite the distance between us and their typical development platform. Connecting with those developers helps us convey the benefits of our products and tools, which, if well exploited, in turn will make their content more efficient, engaging and appealing to their users. And great content makes our products more valuable to our customers and partners.

Nascent verticals such as IoT still offer opportunities to build a direct relationship with developers. When such an opportunity exists, a direct developer outreach approach makes sense. But, in more general terms, we want to access developers further up the stack, while supporting our partners and customers. How can we connect with developers, offer valuable tools and resources, and get them to come back regularly?

An important point is how we measure the success of our efforts. There are obvious metrics, such as sentiment, downloads or followers. These are useful to measure the effect and return of investment of a certain initiative or campaign (did anyone read our blog?, who visited our booth at the event?). The more important, harder to quantify goal is the extent to which we are influencing developers' code to run better on Arm products. There are useful proxies that allow us to gain a sense of the impact, but this would be the subject of a whole new book.

Arm's ecosystem efforts are organised by vertical segments: IoT, Mobile, Automotive, and so on. Regardless of the segment, our approach to the ecosystem is built around some key principles that can be applied horizontally, and are summarized in 4 simple rules, which we will discuss in the rest of the chapter.

Find your angle

Okay, so another company has an outstanding developer program and accesses all the developers you want to reach.

Regardless of that company's ability to connect with their audience - something that you probably don't have any influence upon - it's essential that you identify what it is that you would like to tell the developers that no one else would be able or motivated to do on your behalf. Do you have a tool that provides unique insight? Or especially good coverage for a particular configuration, or use case? Whatever it is, make sure that you can claim ownership of that particular space and be prepared to tell the audience about it.

The question we always ask ourselves is, "would anyone else in the ecosystem be able to do this job better than Arm?". If the answer is no, then we better start working on it.

Implicit in this advice is the fact that you should know your developer audience so well that you can identify a unique opportunity to serve them and, in doing so, raise their awareness of you. This would be obvious in any other field of marketing and for any other product, but when it comes to developers, the 'M' word is almost a taboo, because, as the old adage goes, developers don't like marketing.

Yet developers love a great tool that solves their problems. In our experience, time and resources spent in identifying developers' needs and eliminating their pain points has been hugely valuable. Finding out which tools to build can be achieved formally, through surveys and focus groups with developers, but often a simple conversation with a developer will throw up a lot of useful feedback. Developers love talking about what they don't like in their workflow, especially if they trust that you will do something about it.

Case study 1. Arm Mali graphics and gaming

Despite owning the vast majority of the mobile CPU market, Arm found itself with no significant contact with developers. Mobile is perhaps the most established developer segment, better served by the platform vendors than any other sector in the industry. It would seem that there is very little for Arm to contribute to the developer experience that is not already covered by the two major mobile OS vendors, Google and Apple, or by mobile platforms such as Unity, Facebook, etc.

It was clear to us that we couldn't, and didn't want to, compete with those higher up in the stack. Had we tried to offer an IDE to complete with Android Studio, for example, we would have failed miserably to gain traction - how could we build a better tool than Google? More importantly, it would not have helped support our relationship with Google. And frankly, trying to build something that already exists is not a very exciting challenge. Instead we focused on one area that we found under-served: tools and libraries to debug graphics development on OpenGL ES and Vulkan. There are tools available in the market aimed at profiling graphics applications, but they have several drawbacks for developers of mobile applications. Some are vendor-specific and don't work with other vendors of mobile hardware, while others are too high-level for detailed analysis; in some cases, they lack good integration with the mobile processor, which, in almost every case, is based on an Arm architecture. We realised that we could build a better range of tools to help developers focused on applications with a strong graphic element: mostly games, but increasingly others such as Virtual Reality, Augmented Reality, and so on. This plays to our strengths - we have a very good position in mobile graphics - and complements Google's efforts to provide good solutions for general purpose mobile development.

Even then, there is a difference between deciding to provide competitive development solutions for graphics developers and actually delivering them. The first versions of the tools were too complex. Rather than a minimum viable product, we tried to do everything our customers asked for. With too many moving parts (drivers, operating system, devices, and the tool itself), quality assurance was a challenge and all too often we had reports of users being unable to install or use the tools. We decided to stop developing new features and focus on delivering a great user experience. But user experience is defined by the users, not the development team. To get our tools in order, it took the team multiple interviews with partners, some surveys, and our undivided attention to the problem (see below for a deep dive on this critical aspect). We simplified the product, hiding or removing information that users didn't need.

Better documentation, which was kept up to date, was also essential. However, through interviews with our partners, particularly those in non-English speaking countries, we discovered that that short videos are much more likely to be followed than long online documents, although you need both to supply all the information necessary. We also added integration with other tools into the developer workflow, to make it easier to launch the tool and remove friction. Working with our partners, we encouraged more testing before releasing new versions of the tool or any of the system components. The key was to ensure the first 5 minutes of use are problem-free, otherwise the chances are that you will have lost the user forever. Time for performance profiling is in very short supply, and it cannot be spent just getting the tool to work. We're not quite there yet, but the progress we've made has resulted in more repeated use of our graphics profiling tools by more developers, which will result in better content, more optimized for mobile.

Cultivate talented, credible evangelists

Once you have identified your unique ability to contribute in the ecosystem, you must find developers who are ready to endorse you. The chances are that there are already some developers out there who already know you and love your products. If you have a small team and a shoestring of a budget, you are going to need all the help you can get. It's all about credibility and efficiency.

A credible story comes from developers who believe in your product and think it's worth their time and reputation to endorse it. It's not unusual that a comment in social media from a respected developer receives more retweets or likes than a similar one from the corresponding corporate account.

Efficiency is incredibly important to us due to our smaller size and resource constraints. How do we maximize our efficiency in reaching dozens of different technical segments? The answer is simple: talent. We find the most talented, visionary and dedicated external teams and individuals who are passionate about solving particular problems. Frequently they are technical founders of smaller organizations who tend to be highly motivated to go out and evangelize their solutions to the world.

With tens of billions of Arm-based devices being sold into the market every year, we realize that it is not going to be possible for Arm to hire full-time experts in areas as diverse as medical, drones, robots and aerospace. The most efficient way for us to tell our story is to locate the people who have the most credibility with the developer segments we seek to target and help them accelerate and tell their story, and Arm's, alongside it.

IoT: Arm innovator program

The Arm Innovator Program is a steadily growing group of external technical experts and evangelists with expertise in a broad variety of market segments important to Arm. From a standing start, we have now almost 40 innovators in our program - reaching the limit of what we considered manageable at the onset. Each Arm Innovator is a charismatic evangelist of the products that they have built using Arm technology. We support the Innovators in a variety of ways,including co-marketing, production of proofs-of-concept, workshops, webinars, blog posts, live interviews, hackathons and more.

When executed properly, an Innovator Program can provide explosive opportunities for growth over time. We have found it to be a powerful tool to grow our developer ecosystem and greatly accelerate the innovation occurring on top of Arm technology. We have some examples below where innovators have made a substantial impact in the adoption of our technologies.

This sounds good, but you likely have a few questions such as: How do you locate and identify an Innovator? And what do Innovators get out of working with Arm?

How to identify an innovator

We see Innovators as individuals who build developer experiences on top of other developer experiences. In the case of Arm's microprocessors, an Innovator might be someone who takes an Arm processor, mounts it on a printed circuit board with a specific configuration and then produces the cloud services to turn it into an internet-connected camera to sell into the industrial drainage market. The key characteristic of Innovators is they have intimate knowledge of their own market and can repurpose our technology in a way that we would have not been able to.

Each Innovator provides us with access to developers in a new segment. Furthermore, these Innovators tend to have strong direct market knowledge and can provide interesting feedback to help you improve your own products.

Case study 2: Makerologist and DIY Robocars

In the new field of deep learning, one of the challenges we face at Arm is how to explain to our market that many deep learning and AI tasks can be performed on low-cost Arm hardware without needing to spend huge amounts of money in backend compute power. Because Arm CPUs, Microcontrollers, GPU and other IP are so prolific, if we could educate more developers on the fact that Arm processors can be used for AI, we would be able to create a major impact on the market.

Many developers feel intimidated to prototype and test AI functionality in a way that doesn't require reading white papers or spending huge amounts of time adopting heavy deep learning frameworks. This is where Makerologist and DIY Robocars came in.

When we look to market our products to pools of developers, it is very beneficial to locate communities that have already coalesced around a single niche product or application. With 10,000+ members and 40 global meetups, the DIY Robocars movement to create low-cost autonomous vehicles using Arm technology seemed like a strong fit for our objectives of efficient one-to-many developer marketing efforts. We engaged with Makerologist's Clarissa San Diego and DIY Robocars co-founders Will Roscoe and Adam Conway to launch the very first Seattle DIY Robocars event.

After much planning, we convened 77 developers to build and race 10 DIY Robocars, and were able to attract key AI technical talent from throughout the Seattle region to spend three hours building and racing Robocars and learning about AI on Arm. By embracing fun, community events with Arm Innovators, we were able to achieve high quality in-person connections within the demographics of developers we targeted.

What's in it for the Innovators?

An important characteristic of an Innovator is that they are are small business that is not yet fully established. This is important because the primary motivation of Innovators to work with us is to raise awareness of their product offerings so they can grow larger. Innovators frequently have stockpiles of talent, domain knowledge and motivation. What they lack is exposure.

The goal of a well-run Innovator program is to shine the spotlight directly on each Innovator to give them more opportunities to tell their story. The faster these Innovators move, the more they grow and the more they benefit your company.

We provide wide ranging benefits to our Innovators including funding their workshops, webinars, conference travel, inviting them to special internal Arm events, helping spot fund proof-of-concept ideas and much more. Helping our Innovators grow their market share is directly beneficial to them, and to us.

Case study 3: OpenMV

When Arm Introduced our CMSIS-NN software for deep learning on low-cost microcontrollers, the market quickly forgot the announcement. With an opaque name and highly technical white paper, the true value of the CMSIS-NN libraries was not understandable to many of our developers and not accessible. We sent OpenMV to a small team of just two developers who both have day jobs, a casual one line email mentioning CMSIS-NN and asking them if they could use it. Two weeks later, OpenMV released support for CMSIS-NN on their IoT cameras and demonstrated in a 4 minute video exactly how developers could use the project to create immediate business value.

After circulating the video internally at Arm, we began to be inundated with requests for access to OpenMV and introductions from customers wanting to use the functionality in their own projects immediately. All of this from a two person team and a one line email. This is the value of Arm Innovators, for themselves and the Arm ecosystem.

Leverage partners' channels

As I described at the start of the chapter, we recognise that there are other companies with a closer relationship to developers. Arm's goal is to help those developers build better applications by using the architecture features, tools and best practice, and work with our partners to offer an excellent channel to communicate our value. When the content is relevant and brings actual value to developers, it's in both Arm's and the partner's interest to ensure it reaches the widest audience possible.

This builds brand recognition. If you can, join your partner's booth in an event, or invite them to a webinar. Your audience will recognise their name alongside yours, something particularly important if your name is not well known yet. It's amazing how powerful those associations are, and your brand will be reinforced as a result.

Partner blogs

Arm has a blogging channel in our forum and collaboration site called Arm Community. In our traditional hardware domains, the Community is the place to go to find news and subject experts in the Arm ecosystem. In other areas, such as multimedia software and tools for graphics, its reach is much smaller. When we have content of particular relevance to an audience in those areas - for example, a new algorithm for Virtual or Augmented Reality that offers material benefits for the end user - we try to publish somewhere else outside the Arm Community. Buying sponsored content in a technical publication is an option which works in some cases, but for technical content it can smack of inauthenticity, and you may not have the budget, in any case.

Whenever the piece features some of our partners' technology, a better approach is to try to publish it in their blogging channels. This has worked very well for us. On one occasion, a piece on VR reached 10x the number of views and engagements than we could have possibly achieved in the Arm Community. The partner also benefited with a relevant, engaging and original piece that they would have never have written.

Of course, this approach only works if the partner perceives that the content is going to benefit their pool of users, and the message aligns well with their own. In another instance a different partner refused to publish a similar piece because we were 'hacking' the platform to build a new feature that it wasn't intended for, and which would never be officially supported. It is important to understand, even internalize the partners' developer strategy and objectives, ensuring you are well aligned with them. Your content needs to expand the partner's developer outreach, not take it over.

Put your heart into it

Let's be honest: developers don't have time for us. They are busy getting their product out of the door, or responding to a demanding customer. They will not become your beta testers free of charge, or be expected to take something that almost solves a problem and have to figure out what's missing, filling the gaps themselves. If you have identified your angle - what it is that you can do for developers better than anyone else - it doesn't matter how big or small, broad or narrow, make sure that you can solve that particular problem completely, and do it better than anything else in the market. Think about whether your enthusiastic developer evangelists will shout about it, and whether your partners will be happy to promote it in their channels. If you don't think you can delight your users, don't waste your time on it. It will fail to rise to the surface amongst the rest of less-than-ideal solutions out there.

Case study 4: mobile compute with Arm NEON

Not all mobile applications are the same. In compute-intensive tasks such as sound or vision processing, or machine learning, developers need to make the most of the hardware available to them. In 2010, Arm started to include a vectorized engine called NEON in their CPUs. A few years later, virtually every mobile application processor is NEON-accelerated.

Modern compilers do a reasonably good job of optimising code for available NEON hardware, but they won't achieve the optimum performance for a given routine. In those cases where compiler output is not enough, it is necessary to optimize the code by hand, or have someone else do it for you.

Ne10 was Arm's first attempt to create a developer answer to the need for optimised NEON code, in the form of a library of primitive functions for applications such as computer vision. In 2011, a few engineers set out to build an open source project that would combine some of the most commonly used primitives in compute-intensive applications, opening a hosting page and sharing it with their contacts in the industry. Despite a promising start and a good degree of excitement amongst partners, Ne10 ultimately failed to live up to the principle of putting your heart to it: the library was incomplete, providing only some functionality that the user was expected to complement with their own. In addition, it was not very well documented and in some cases not as well optimized as other open source functions already available. While the library enjoyed some success in certain computer vision communities and research labs, it eventually fell out of official maintenance and now only survives in GitHub thanks to the contributions of a small number of individual industry advocates.

Building on the learnings of Ne10, Arm released its new compute library in 2017. This time we considered it to be a central element of our success in mobile compute. A product owner travelled the world for over a year meeting with tens of developers and partners to understand their needs, and prioritized work based on it. A team was set up to work on the project full time and support ongoing requests and issues, creating a careful outreach plan to ensure that the benefits and repository updates were clearly communicated to the developer audience. The library was embraced not only by the mobile business unit at Arm, but by many others, such as embedded and automotive; and so on. Since it was launched, the Compute Library has become the most starred project amongst the more than 60 open source Arm repositories in Github. Today it still has a team working on this library full time and has added other key use cases besides computer vision, such as deep learning, to the list of functions optimized by the library. Thanks to this work the team has been able to engage with a large number of new developers, building trust and gaining access to new opportunities for growth.

Summary

Whilst every company would love to have a developer program that reaches millions of passionate advocates, unless you have bottomless pockets, it's unlikely that you will ever be in that position. However that doesn't mean you should give up your developer program, or that you should settle for a vague sense that people are aware of you and your product.

With a systematic approach to understanding your value proposition, your audience and the developer landscape, it's possible to find a unique angle that both your developers and your partners will love to endorse and promote, amplifying many times any effort you could make on your own. They key is to put all of your energy into identifying your angle and then committing to it for the long term.

Chapter 9 | Hardware Is The New Software - Building A Developer Community Around A Chip Instead Of An SDK

Ana Schafer: Director of Product Marketing - Qualcomm Technologies, Inc.
Christine Jorgensen: Director of Product Marketing - Qualcomm Technologies, Inc.

You are the head of developer relations for a program that has been focused on software development. Now, you are tasked with building a community around a solution that requires programming and building in the physical world with a combination of hardware and software. What's different about marketing to software developers versus hardware developers anyway? And what is different when it comes to events, support, content and logistics? How do you acquire, educate, engage and retain hardware developers? How do you continually drive toward commercialization for yourself, your developers and everyone in your ecosystem?

Whether your goal is to start a developer community from the ground up or encourage your existing developer community to follow you into new areas and opportunities - or a little of both - this chapter is for you.

Introduction

At Qualcomm Technologies, Inc., we create many of the inventions behind wireless communication, and we've been facing these questions in our efforts to get our technologies into the hands of more developers in different areas. As our company's business strategy takes us beyond smartphones, we're focused on encouraging developers to work with our new hardware, which leads to two main developer marketing goals: encouraging a large community of mobile app developers, who already know us, and attracting an even larger community of hardware developers who are new to us.

This chapter describes how we introduced a new hardware development tool - the DragonBoard™ 410c - a small, single-board computer that is accessible to almost any software or hardware developer and compliant with an open-source hardware specification. It is designed to ease developer engagement with our technologies by allowing developers to prototype and invent in myriad directions, supporting our growth in Internet of Things (IoT) and opening the door to brand-new use cases. Critical to the adoption of the DragonBoard 410c has been a focus on making hardware the new software: accessible, affordable, expandable and easily programmable.

The task for our marketing team at Qualcomm Developer Network (QDN) was to build a community of followers ranging from our longtime, multinational customers, to newcomer startups, makers and educators. Along the way, we learnt some lessons about developer marketing around hardware, which we'll share as we describe the journey.

New business opportunities beckon

Long before the term "Internet of Things" became a staple in our vocabulary, our product management team had been making development boards built around our mobile processors, populated with the connectors and physical interfaces needed by component vendors to integrate their hardware into smartphones using our processors. As companies began exploring the combination of computing and wireless connectivity in new applications, manufacturers in a wide variety of industries saw potential for our processors far beyond smartphones. Qualcomm Technologies began fielding requests for development boards to evaluate use of our mobile processors in areas such as robotics, drones, home automation, appliances, toys and media servers. The opportunity was clear, but our company needed to build a new commercialization approach as we diversified our business.

In the Internet of Things, most embedded systems have modest product requirements compared to mobile communication devices like smartphones and tablets, and Qualcomm® Snapdragon™ processors[1] meet the most important of these such as high performance, low power consumption, and wireless connectivity.

However, we had to build a new commercialization strategy for IoT that met the requirements of an array of embedded devices that, for example, have a much longer lifespan compared to the typical, one to two year lifespan of most smartphones. Other requirements included an ecosystem of hardware vendors who could provide off-the-shelf or custom modules as well as system integration services, and a mature distribution channel to scale from dozens to thousands of customers. Customers would also require an evaluation board, and our approach was to provide an open source, low-cost (under $100) community development board for potential customers to evaluate our processors.

To meet these needs, Qualcomm Technologies focused on the Snapdragon 410E (http://sdata.me/RuZDzs), a mobile processor optimized for mass production in IoT, and alongside it, an easily accessible prototyping platform, the DragonBoard 410c (https://sdata.me/XgqRgw), a development board compliant with an established open hardware specification, accompanied by product information and support resources. The business goal was that developers would use the DragonBoard 410c to build prototype designs that they could then commercialize in products based on the Snapdragon 410E processor by using off-the-shelf modules, or purchase the processor for a chip-on-board designs.

While the product team worked on rolling out the DragonBoard 410c, the developer marketing team set its own wheels in motion. Before long, we encountered our first speed bumps.

---

[1] Qualcomm Snapdragon is a product of Qualcomm Technologies, Inc. and/or its subsidiaries.

At Qualcomm Developer Network, our focus had previously always been on mobile software developers. However, we now needed to build a strong, engaged community of both hardware and software developers around the DragonBoard 410c. We had many years of experience working with smartphone engineers, but we needed to target developers in a broad array of new and emerging IoT segments.

The smartphone business involves a very small number of very large customers, each one with a Research and Development group staffed by experienced engineers. The nascent IoT business, on the other hand, involves a large number of relatively small customers many with a tiny R&D staff, if any, often flying by the seat of their pants to invent first-time devices with features nobody knows they need yet.

Defining the target audience - where to start?

The product plan for the Snapdragon 410E processor was to let a thousand flowers bloom: to make it as easy as possible to use, to build up a broad community and channel, then see where biggest leads came from and tune the business approach along the way. That's a difficult place for developer marketing to work.

"Who is our target audience?" we asked. "Lots of people," the product team told us.

"What will they make with the board?" "Lots of things. You know, for the Internet of Things."

"Can you identify a few key vertical segments to focus on for our initial campaigns?" "Why would we do that? We need to position the product as broadly as possible."

Not exactly the well-defined target audience and clear direction we all hope for, was it?

But that was inherent to the position Snapdragon 410E held in the Qualcomm Technologies IoT portfolio as a product that could broadly apply across existing and emerging use cases. It was a challenging situation to start building a developer marketing plan with high-volume aspirations and such a wide net as the product team was directing us to cast. We started by researching global developer trends as well as our own community. As you'll see throughout the rest of this chapter, tuning in to the voice of the developer was not only a good place to start, but also looking back, the tactics that proved to be most valuable during those early days of product introduction were the ones that elicited the most direct developer feedback.

Researching the space - starting our developer marketing plan

We had a strong, existing community of mobile app developers exploring IoT, but we also wanted to reach beyond that base to attract experienced hardware developers to the Qualcomm Developer Network for the first time. So, as every marketing team facing such a transition should do, we researched the differences between software developer communities and hardware developer communities.

First, we evaluated the type and quality of resources (documentation, sample code, projects, content, support) that other companies provided their hardware communities. Then we reviewed market research from sources like SlashData, comparing it to the annual survey we conduct within our own developer community. Several elements stood out:

- Developers were becoming more conscious that hardware was increasing in power and decreasing in price. The lower barrier to entry was feeding a flourishing community of hardware startups and makers ready to engage with vendors.

- Interest and expertise in programming were rising among makers, academics and entrepreneurs, outside of traditional developer circles.

- Developers were looking beyond established areas and technologies to the next ones, such as IoT, either to keep their skills up to date or to probe new sources of revenue.

- Developers were starting to place greater value on professional skill building and continuous education provided by developer programs.

- To analysts, IoT looked like a huge, wide-open frontier. To developers trying to figure out where to sink their shovel, it looked like a confusing landscape of relatively small, vertical markets. They saw a fragmented group of software and hardware solutions vying for their attention, with few unifying standards to use as a compass.

133

Weighing all these factors together we decided to prioritize educational content creation over promotional spends in the early stages. The developer marketing team had long since learned the lesson that comes from promoting an SDK or developer tool that has inadequate documentation. You may drive visitors to the landing page, but the number of downloads and follow-on uses will be low. We knew we had to make building with our hardware as easy as programming software if it was going to be a vehicle for developers taking their first steps into IoT and quickly prototyping new designs. Educational content would be key to making this new space accessible.

Hardening the product and encouraging community feedback

From researching the developer community and commercialization requirements, we knew that we didn't yet have everything we wanted for launch, but we didn't want the perfect to become the enemy of the good. Besides, our experience told us that once we had released the DragonBoard 410c, the community would let us know what was lacking and how to improve it.

We generated the educational content with which we would roll out the board, knowing the list would grow and change with time. In startup parlance, our minimum viable product content for launch was as follows:

- Documentation starting off with a hardware user manual, data sheet and application notes
- Getting started projects that include step by step building instructions
- Sample code to quickly program different functions
- Short tutorial videos specific to an application.

With baseline product content in place, we then had the foundation for creating the marketing content to evangelize the product and drive calls to action to the educational resources:

- Blog posts using a three-stage editorial approach on a theme, starting with beginner-level and ending in expert blogs on technology applications, vertical uses cases, and so on

- Monthly Newsletters with project of the month feature - a feature story pulled from the blogs to highlight the new resources
- Webinars hosted with key software and hardware providers in the ecosystem
- Use cases based on commercial applications.

The community gave us good feedback about our educational content: it was insufficient; sometimes too fluffy, sometimes too far advanced. We started gathering our feedback by monitoring the questions in the forums, and as we started participating in hackathons we found these to be an even more valuable source for developer feedback. With developers working under such tight time constraints, we could immediately see what was easy to follow and where things were lacking or totally missing.

Early on, we had turned to our company's internal resources and to our vendor ecosystem for documentation. In most cases, it had been written by savvy engineers for savvy engineers and assumed too much foundational knowledge for the broad audience we were approaching. Over time, when we thought we had addressed much of the feedback and that our resources were really solid, we turned from doing hackathons that targeted mostly professional developers to Major League Hacking, which put us in front of thousands of university students and gave our content its biggest trial by fire. We got a rude awakening about how many leaps in knowledge our content took, and it was only after we started providing level-appropriate resources and sample code that we began to see a strong number of completed projects from the hackathons. The takeaway points to share from that experience are that you should always be open to feedback from the community, as there will be different insights from each new audience you reach out to. It is easy to become complacent when there are so many glaring needs vying for your attention.

Starting at home

Before we took the DragonBoard 410c to its first hackathon, we reached out to our own internal engineering community. Our company is filled with lots of engineering talent, but our developer marketing team struggles for access to technical staff the same way most developer programs do. There are always important customers commanding priority and product schedules that can't be missed. We didn't have assigned resources to help developer marketing create sample code and educational content for the DragonBoard 410c, so we invited our engineers to play with it.

Our product team vigorously promoted the DragonBoard 410c to engineers companywide, seeding hundreds of boards through an internal mailing list. The "DragonBoard Club" sprouted up, consisting of engineers who, in their personal time, are hobbyists or are involved in promoting science-technology-engineering-math (STEM) education through alumni programs and school volunteer programs, such as high school robotics clubs. This group of passionate engineers spanned San Diego and San Jose, California; Research Triangle Park, North Carolina; Toronto, Canada; Cambridge, UK; and Hyderabad, India.

What was in it for them? We rewarded employees who created projects, wrote documentation or provided support at hackathons with formal recognition awards for accomplishments that went above and beyond their normal day-to-day job, plus they were able to keep their boards at no charge. But the main motivation for the DragonBoard Club members was their love for tinkering.

What was in it for us? The DragonBoard Club contributed broadly in several important ways by:

- Testing the board and the quality of initial educational resources

- Creating demos, workshops and video tutorials that developers would ultimately use

- Evangelizing the board by sharing it with alumni groups and high school clubs

- Identifying the features and functions that would be most inspiring to developers (computer vision rated very highly)

- Documenting our earliest projects

Their contribution of creating and documenting projects was invaluable. In the same way that case studies and customer testimonials enhance the credibility of every business, published projects are the vehicle by which hardware platforms like Raspberry Pi and Arduino demonstrate credibility to their communities, encouraging other developers to not only draw inspiration from prior work but also replicate and improve upon it.

By starting at home, we in developer marketing were able to publicize successful DragonBoard 410c projects on the Qualcomm Developer Network website early on. Projects include a description, source code, bills of materials, assembly instructions, and often videos of the project in action, and are classified by categories like hardware, operating system, area of focus and, most important, skill level. We recognize that our community is wide-ranging in experience and areas of specialization, and we've continually tuned our resources to address both the experienced hardware developer and the beginner.

Over time and with much nurturing, we got to the point where community members are contributing their own projects unsolicited, which is a key metric for product engagement.

Driving awareness

Through traditional marketing communications techniques, we maintain a steady drumbeat of awareness and education to draw new developers into our funnel. Registered Qualcomm Developer Network developers receive email notifications of new resources in areas of interest, social media campaigns drive visits to our website, and our monthly newsletter has proven the most effective tactic to drive blog readership.

We also exhibit at events, such as Maker Faire (https://sdata.me/VeHzuk). We're well aware that many makers still don't know who Qualcomm Technologies is, and many more still don't know that the DragonBoard 410c is an open-spec development kit designed to be as powerful as a smartphone. Shows like Maker Faire that attract the T-shirt vs. sports coat and jeans crowd are a rich opportunity for driving awareness and education, as we get access to an audience that is interested in diving into the technology behind our demos and engaging directly with the engineers in the booth.

Our biggest reach in driving global awareness in our early days came from the DragonBoard 410c Maker Month Contest. We announced the contest and challenged developers worldwide to submit ideas of what they would build if they had a DragonBoard 410c. Almost 800 ideas came in from all over the world — from a testing device for foodborne pathogens to an under-vehicle device for mapping potholes, and everything in between. Then, importantly, we asked our entire developer network to judge the ideas and vote on them. More than 17,000 developers voted on the ideas, and the top 31 ideas won the first round. We shipped a free DragonBoard 410c to each of the first-round winners, giving them one month to build their proposed invention and send us video showing it at work. A small panel of judges, consisting of our engineers and channel and distribution members, then selected a final winner and awarded the grand prize of $5,000.

We believe that having the developer community vote for the first-round winners was an important element in the success of the contest. The conversations it started among developers all over the globe spread awareness of the DragonBoard 410c and educated prospective makers on its uniqueness as an open-spec development kit with the processing power of a smartphone. The contest also provided a huge boost to our projects page, as we posted the instructions from many of the first-round winners to inspire imitation and innovation.

From awareness to engagement - hardware hackathons

For many years, we have used hackathons as a vehicle for engaging developers with software products and we were keen to continue tapping into the creative energy the events are known for. However, we soon discovered that pulling off a successful hardware hackathon was a big step beyond.

For software hackathons we generally provide documentation, code samples and a software development kit (SDK). Since these are online resources available from anywhere in the world, there are few physical resources to transport. In contrast, almost everything related to a hardware hackathon involves physical equipment, so the hack kits we prepared for each team required much more preparation, transportation, logistics, support, and sometimes export/import arrangements.

Our first hackathon was a bit of an eye-opener on what it would take to make hardware as easy to program as software. We participated in TechCrunch Disrupt and found that attendees skewed toward software-oriented; those with hardware experience knew Arduino but not a full computing platform, and the DragonBoard 410c at this point did not have a strong complement of plug in mezzanine boards. Those who wanted to connect sensors had the additional burden of dealing with breadboards, level shifters, and soldering irons - not exactly what many of the software developers wanted to spend their time on. Subsequently, most of the projects they ended up submitting were little more than Android apps running on the DragonBoard 410c. We learned that besides the hack kit we provided, we needed to make all of the hardware components for IoT (e.g. sensors and cameras) more accessible, and we needed to provide lots of sample code and projects to allow developers to take advantage of the board's capabilities.

Developers also needed live, on-site hardware expertise. There is no substitute for an engineer who knows the board and can answer any kind of question face-to-face at half past midnight. Naturally, it took some doing to pull our engineers away from their desks (and weekends) for hackathon duty, although we benefited yet again from the strength of our internal DragonBoard club, but the effort paid off in better projects and more-satisfied developers.

An important goal for the hackathons was to demonstrate that the more things the DragonBoard 410c can easily connect to and work with, the more valuable it becomes for the developer. As we gained traction and our hardware ecosystem expanded, we were able to include purpose-built mezzanine boards and plug-and-play sensors into the hack kits. Those components allowed hackers to focus on program logic and use cases without the tedium of attaching wires to pins.

We also learned the importance of targeting more hardware-focused hackathons in order to engage with the right audience for our products. While limiting the number of events we participated in (since many hackathons are software-focused), we received a far better return on our investment in time and resources. Along the way we also learned more valuable lessons about laying the groundwork for a successful event, particularly from our sponsorship at the AT&T Developer Conference:

- Use cases - Whether we are emphasizing multimedia, computer vision, edge computing or any other use for the DragonBoard 410c, we try to tailor our hackathon challenge, and our hack kit, to align with that event's focus.

- Co-sponsors - By finding out in advance which devices, SDKs, or cloud providers the event co-sponsors planned to highlight we are able to cross-promote the DragonBoard 410c with sensors, cameras and services like AT&T M2X.

- Pre-hackathon webinars. A couple of weeks before the event, we like to reach out to the attendees with a webinar in which our engineers walk through the capabilities of the DragonBoard 410c and the contents of the hack kit.

- Resources - Hackathons leave little time for combing through documentation, so we come prepared with easy-to-follow code, shortcuts, sample projects and video tutorials aligned with the main themes of the event, highlight these during the pre-hackathon webinar and make them easily accessible on a hack-specific resource page on our website.

- Hackathon teams - Experienced hackers arrive as a team with an idea of what they want to build and the categories in which they want to compete. In addition to trying to capture the interest of teams in the pre-hack webinar, we send our staff out to promote our challenge throughout the registration time showing off all the goodies in the hack kit to increase uptake with high-value hackers.

Hackathons and similar live events play a big role in our engagement with the hardware community. Developers like these events and the atmosphere of innovation that pervades them. Although submitted hack projects tend to be more science experiment than useful commercial applications, with the approach outlined in this section we've been able to uncover some gems. Most importantly, we find them to be a great way of fueling developer awareness and interest in a new technology, and a valuable testing ground for continually making the DragonBoard 410c easier to use. We've hosted winning teams and their DragonBoard 410c projects in our booth at subsequent trade shows, including a grand prize winner that prototyped a home health automation system, increasing their exposure and ours.

Smart companies start small - for example, conducting local workshops for meetup groups or mini-hackathons with your company's summer interns - then collect the feedback they need to run large events with hundreds of attendees. Hackathons reveal what developers can do with technologies and devices, but they are not the shortest, or easiest path to achieving solid business goals. Also, hosting your own hackathon can be very expensive in terms of time and dollars, so it is often best to seek out existing well-known and well-attended hackathons that align with your business goals by looking closely at the demographic details from previous events, as well as the published entrants and winning hacks.

Building retention through commercial success

As we progressed towards a strong foundation with more and better documentation, sample code, projects, etc., and as we continued to build our hardware developer community, we knew we needed to align our growth with our goals for commercial success. The time was right to examine our approach to driving commercial wins in targeted use cases, and in doing so we had to acknowledge that in the world of IoT, our hardware is just one piece of what a potential customers would consider in an entire end-to-end commercial solution. The same is probably true for most developer programs, whatever the offering you are marketing, it is just one element in what your end customers would need to get to a final commercial product. For us, turning to our ecosystem for collaboration in developer marketing and enablement was a great area of opportunity in driving uptake in specific commercial applications.

Co-marketing with the ecosystem - a virtuous cycle

From the beginning, we designed the DragonBoard 410c to be compatible with the 96Boards Consumer Edition specification, an open standard that reassures inventors that they can develop prototypes without being locked in to any single vendor's architecture. This standard also meant that hardware vendors making add-on shields, or what 96Boards calls mezzanines, with their components (sensors, motors, displays, cameras, cellular modems, etc.) were able to support all 96Boards single board computers, including the DragonBoard. The result was a quickly expanding hardware ecosystem of components, in addition to the module ecosystem the product team had developed.

141

As the landscape widened to areas like machine learning, network edge and cloud computing, we also expanded our ecosystem to include software and cloud providers who can help us gain a better foothold in these areas. For example, the combination of on-device computing with wireless and cloud connectivity has become an important factor in most targeted opportunities, so we have published DragonBoard 410c projects for major cloud services including AWS IoT and AWS Greengrass, IBM Bluemix, IBM Watson IoT, AT&T M2X, and Microsoft Azure IoT.

In order to translate this ecosystem of hardware and software providers into commercial implementations, we developed win-win developer co-marketing opportunities with this community to inspire designs in targeted use cases. We turned to the ecosystem to solve the problem of how to get technical content and resources to inspire design-in, and in exchange offered valuable promotional opportunities to reach the growing community engaged with Qualcomm Developer Network. For example, we worked with Solstice, an IT services firm, who developed a facilities management demo on DragonBoard 410c with AWS Greengrass, and in exchange we showcased it in our booth at AWS re:Invent, highlighted it as a project, and featured the use case in a blog and did a profile of the lead developer in our Developer of the Month. Another example is our work with Timesys, a firm specializing in Linux development services, who created a four-part webinar series we hosted on developing for industrial IoT with Linux OS using an industrial gateway as their use case. The results were strong leads for Timesys, strong leads for us and, most importantly, a satisfied technical audience.

In engaging with new ecosystem members on co-marketing we worked to customize our approach based on mutual goals, but following is the list of possible engagements we typically started with:

- Guest blogs
- 'Developer of the Month' feature
- Posting of ecosystem project
- Hosted webinars with ecosystem company speaker
- Feature in monthly newsletter

- Hack kit loaners for ecosystem-hosted events
- Demo placement in Qualcomm booth at industry events.

We continue to nurture our developer community and ecosystem through the ongoing marketing program that reaches out to our database of engaged developers, and in exchange the hardware and software companies we work with have provided the expertise that our developers want, which has taught us valuable lessons about reciprocity and the ecosystem.

Summing it up

Here are some of the main takeaways from our developer marketing experiences in building a developer community around hardware:

- Start with what you know and do your research for what hardware developers need and want, namely quality documentation, sample code, and support. Be open to feedback on what you provide.

- When hardening a product and developing resources, start small and with a community you know so there is very open, direct feedback and they are invested in your success. In our case it was our internal DragonBoard club of engineers who love to tinker that kick-started a big part of our initial resources.

- It may still be a while before "hardware is as easy to program as software," but nevertheless, that has been an extremely useful theme for our work with the DragonBoard 410c. Almost everything we've done has supported the objective of helping people prototype their ideas and get to commercial viability as quickly as possible.

- While we started off without the well-defined target audience and use cases we would have preferred, we were hopeful that simply getting the DragonBoard 410c into the hands of the community would be a catalyst to help gain valuable feedback, and focus. By turning our attention outward and looking for patterns in what developers were making and asking for, we were able to adjust our approach to drive early successes.

- With time and more initial projects, however, we learned an important lesson: What users were making was not as significant as the DragonBoard 410c features they were using to make it. We saw them create IoT projects that took advantage of the board's smartphone-caliber technologies like camera, multimedia, gesture recognition and especially computer vision. Some users even took the DragonBoard 410c into hub and gateway applications. This feature interest directly fed our requirements for reference applications, sample code and documentation.

- Since educational content is so key for developers, we continue to look for, adapt, translate or create documentation with the instruction level and context that developers need to prototype their designs quickly.

- The ecosystem is more than a pool of customers and vendors; it is a pool of potential solutions. Whether relying on our developer community to promote and judge our contest entries or turning to our ecosystem of distributors, hardware and software vendors for technical capacity we couldn't get internally, we've enjoyed huge ROI from our relationships.

We continuously review and refine efforts, keeping in mind the entire developer journey from awareness, education, engagement and retention, to examine what's working and what's not. We think of each of our outreaches as an integrated 360° marketing campaign to get the most momentum of every event, hackathon, webinar, promoting and pushing through blogs, newsletters, projects, and social media.

Chapter 10 | Behind The Scenes Of Great Developer Events

Katherine Miller: Lead, Cloud Developer Relations Events Program - Google

Events are a core part of many companies' developer marketing plans, and attending in-person activities are central to many developers' professional and personal experiences. Survey data shows, however, that they are considered by developers to be overfunded compared to other programs.

How can one reconcile budget priorities and investment in events with what is important to developers? The answer is relatively simple. Events can be a platform through which to directly connect developers to the experiences and program features they most value in an authentic and measurable manner. By focusing on training, access to experts, labs, and support, events are less entities unto themselves, and more concentrated, multi-program marketing campaigns.

This chapter will focus on how to successfully plan and execute developer events to raise awareness of highly valued tools and programs, optimizing their return on investment - not only in the eyes of finance - but also in the eyes of the developer audience.

Different events serve different purposes. For the purpose of this discussion, events may include:

- Marquee company-level or product-level events with thousands of attendees such as Google I/O, Dreamforce, or WWDC.

- Broad product area events and trade shows such as O'Reilly's Strata or Velocity events, which also attract attendees in the hundreds to low thousands, although may be smaller in scale than those above.

- Language or technology-specific shows such as Kubecon/CNCF, RubyConf, JavaOne.

- Community-driven events such as DevFests, DevOpsDays.

- Local meetups, which may involve tens to low hundreds of attendees.

The objectives and tactics discussed in this chapter apply generally across event types; if something is ideal for a particular type of event, it is called out specifically.

Introduction

According to SlashData's Q3 2017 Developer Benchmark Report, only 11% of respondents ranked Meetups as a top-five developer program feature; conferences and trade shows were lower still at 10%. Conferences and trade shows, however, were ranked highest in terms of budget priorities, and meetups were also a higher budget priority than they were of importance to developers.

On the other hand, activities such as training courses and certifications (36%), access to experts (22%) and hands-on labs (21%) were ranked in the top 5 by a higher percentage of respondents, and are often considered by developers to be the critical elements of meetups, conferences and trade shows.

Upon reviewing this data, should we as marketing professionals simply dismiss events? On the contrary, so long as we target events to be part of larger, focused marketing initiatives, we can use them effectively to build positive brand affinity, humanize companies, provide direct opportunities for networking and professional growth, and be significant sources of reusable content.

Why Events?

What is it about events that makes them a compelling tactic in the developer marketing toolkit? At their core, events play a key role in engaging with one's target audience because they present opportunities for attendees to:

- Connect with like-minded people from the host company or wider community
- Build relationships and network with one another
- Deliver meaningful, constructive product feedback.

Events can also inspire, drive awareness and adoption, and offer easily accessible training and support.

The impact of an event is easy to dismiss and difficult to measure, thereby doesn't have a demonstrable return on investment to match its level of budget prioritization. However, with thoughtfulness and carefully planned data collection integrated upfront, events can yield meaningful, measurable information.

My journey to developer marketing and events took me through a number of industries and roles. Through early career experiences, though, such as hosting prospective students at a dental school, networking with advertisers at a reception, or engaging with agency leadership about product strategy, I realized the business impact that comes from bringing people together to learn, build relationships, solve problems and gain trust.

This passion, and the opportunity to use years of sales, marketing and event experience across industries with a new audience, led me to Developer Marketing at Google. Since 2012, I've led multiple work streams for marquee events such as Google I/O and Google Cloud Next, and built out global developer social media efforts, including processes for incorporating social media into events. I currently lead the Cloud Developer Relations (DevRel) events program, which focuses on how to enable DevRel to most effectively use events to achieve its objectives.

The information shared in this chapter reflects what I have learned through my experiences. The ideas expressed are mine alone, and not those of Google or the other companies for which I have worked. Likewise, I am not promoting or endorsing any specific tools. Anything mentioned is from personal experience, and decisions should be made based on budget and individual assessment.

I owe much to my Developer Relations and Developer Marketing colleagues throughout the industry, who have nurtured my knowledge of and passion for the space, and whose wisdom and insight have helped inform my practice of developer event management, and the tips shared in this chapter.

Delivering valuable, scalable and repeatable events

On reflecting upon my own journey through developer events, paired with live-event social media conversations, press cycles, and post-event surveys, I've found that successful events (of any size) deliver content seen as deeply valuable to the audience. In addition, the "extended" elements which accompany them scale the reach of the programming to have even greater impact beyond the physical event. Below I'll review what I've observed has (or has not) worked, and why.

"Serve up deep technical content"

I hear this feedback from attendees consistently, no matter how many more demos are included or code samples shared. I once pressed a product management lead to articulate what "deep technical content" truly meant, and they reflected that the best technical sessions leave the average audience attendee understanding approximately 2/3 of the content. Ideally, they are engaged, see the opportunity, and understand the next steps, yet are challenged to head home and dig into something new and unfamiliar.

The steps taken to deliver this most successfully have included engaging Developer Relations experts (advocates, engineers and technical writers alike) to advise on content strategy early in the planning process. For example, give them the opportunity to select sessions and demos, and be deeply involved in the content creation. Their core roles focus on driving awareness, learning, adoption and feedback through accessible, user-friendly resources, such as technical demos, videos, articles, presentations, samples and getting started materials. These Developer Relations experts are thus uniquely placed to drive and influence an event's content strategy.

Connecting this back to valued developer programs, technical content at events may include multiple pedagogies, such as presentations, panels, and instructor-led training courses and certification. In addition - budget-depending - recording sessions at events has been a way to scalably create an extensive repository of instructional video content. For this to succeed, it's critical to have a strong production team, a robust content curation and promotion plan, and the ability to post videos live as quickly as possible once the sessions conclude.

Do not sell to developers

"Welcome to developer marketing. You cannot market to developers". So how can we drive developers to use our company's technology without coming across as too "marketing-y" or "sales-y?" I've approached this in a number of different ways:

- **Creating physical space for authentic conversations** - whether it be a meet up lounge at a large event, or a booth at a trade show, the right space design can create the "hallway track." Different configurations invite audiences of varying levels of awareness and engagement:

  o demo stands and lightning talk spaces draw people into the space

  o hands on labs spaces encourage learning and Q&A

  o highboy tables welcome 1:few discussions

  o reconfigurable stools accommodate larger groups.

Learn how to design with consideration for physical accessibility, as well as how to achieve multiple goals in constrained spaces. It's critical to set clear priorities up front to ensure focused, accessible spaces.

- **Having experts available** - in addition to thoughtful space design, trust and authenticity can be accomplished by including technical experts in the planning and staffing of an event. While titles and roles may vary, success can be achieved by involving individuals who are willing and able to not only advocate on behalf of an organization, but also on behalf of the developer. In addition, commit to listening to, documenting and passing along constructive product feedback. This also satisfies the desire for access to experts.

Identifying people to work at an event can pose a challenge, particularly if it requires travel, if you are a lean organization, or if events are not part of the company culture. Confirm staffing commitment from relevant teams before deciding on the type and size of event to plan (there's nothing more stressful than scrambling for staff last minute. While this may be inevitable, the level of stress can be minimized with upfront commitments).

Request help from individuals enough in advance for them to arrange their schedules and book affordable travel. Don't assume that people attending the event for other reasons (such as speaking or customer meetings) will be able to cover staffing duties. Connecting events to greater developer program goals, ensuring there's a measurement plan, and positioning the work as core to one's job function can help mitigate these challenges. Another approach to this is running fewer, yet highly targeted events to optimize the availability of in-person resources.

Create meaningful ways for attendees to connect with one another

Standard practices for connecting may include receptions and "birds of a feather" gatherings with individuals of similar backgrounds and interests. While not particularly innovative on the surface, applying a standard and well-established approach has made a significant difference in their effectiveness. For "birds of a feather" engagements and other community-oriented activities, success has come when their promotion has been deeply integrated into the event website and comms strategy. Without this thoughtful integration, these activities may feel like an "add on," and may not be as successful due to lack of awareness.

At a reception, thoughtfulness on food and beverage queueing systems, seating arrangements, and choices makes people feel more welcome and relaxed. While many of the learnings may seem obvious, we can all reflect back on well-intentioned events that missed one or more of these best practices, and resulted in sub-par experiences.

Have enough food and drink stations so that people do not need to wait in long queues awkwardly holding a glass, swag, and small, precariously balanced plates (and missing out on valuable socialization time). Make it clear in the invitation whether a meal will be provided, or if it'll be appetizers or dessert only (this way people can plan any additional dining accordingly). Intersperse highboys with lower tables and chairs for both accessibility as well as to accommodate people who wish to move about or wish to enjoy a more leisurely conversation. Ensure that there is ample food (there's nothing worse than running out of food), and sufficient selections for people of all dietary needs (protip - ask for dietary needs in the RSVP! Endeavour to provide non-alcoholic options beyond water and soda - and if there are signature drinks, create one that is non-alcoholic).

When outdoors, planning ahead for potential extreme weather conditions allows for greater comfort. If it's in a season with greatly variable temperatures, incorporate shade into a space, as well as have throw blankets and heat lamps on hand. Is there a chance of precipitation? Consider a space that isn't fully outdoors. Have bug spray and sunscreen available. When indoors, think through whether it's a conversation-driven event or a free-flowing party, and plan music choices and volume accordingly, setting the right expectations and minimizing frustrations.

For any of these, show thoughtfulness to the small gestures. Personalized name tags that allow people to share their passions, group activities such as photo booths or photo walls or "How May I?" exercises, custom shirts or pins for people to proudly express their identities. These all go a long way towards driving connectivity and a sense of belonging. If planning events globally, collaborate with colleagues in that region to incorporate in gestures that best resonate with local audiences.

Be honest and targeted

It is easy to focus on the innovation angle, particularly for the potential impact of "magic moments" on brand and press. But what may be magic from a traditional brand perspective may seem gimmicky or inauthentic to developers (how many times have we all been told that something is too "marketing-y" or "sales-y?"). Developers don't just want a slide presentation. They want to see code, touch code and break code.

In many ways, then, the magic is in showing how the innovation presents opportunity and that the developers behind the technology are trustworthy, authentic and humble. For example, not overpromising on the experience, not being afraid to have things break on stage, and being OK with feedback. Success has come from demos that truly reflect how the technology works (even with its limitations). It also comes from sponsorship sizes that reflect the story ready to be told, and a focus on content and programming that match the audience.

Show commitment to diversity and inclusion

An imperative learning to highlight on the journey is to make diversity and inclusion planning core to the event planning. Having it as its own category of content or programming can come across as lip service and not true investment. The aim should be to "show" not "tell" the audience you are committed to being diverse and inclusive, and that your event just is that way inherently. By making an event (and by way of that, the tools and programs promoted within the event), accessible and inclusive, it will broaden the reach and impact of the experience.

Strategies I've seen be successful include:

- Attention to who is speaking, and action taken to seek out and encourage participation from a range of individuals, rather than waiting to see who submits a proposal, and shrugging off a lack of diversity if few are received from typically under-represented groups. Also, if you do reach out proactively, don't make it seem like you're reaching out because that person is an underrepresented minority (URM) (e.g. "we want more women at our conference so can you come and speak?"). Instead let them know that they are an expert in X subject and you would love to have them share their knowledge.

- Thoughtfulness around images in decks and other marketing materials. People want to see themselves, and don't want to see stereotypes, such as groups comprising just "brogrammers", exacerbated.

- Having a well-publicized code of conduct and an escalation path for attendees who are not treated properly at the event, such as Google's Event Community Guidelines and Anti-Harassment Policy https://sdata.me/sukUxE or the Salesforce Event Code of Conduct https://sdata.me/SmlNbq.

- Developing a strong acquisition strategy to reach into under-represented communities, including through partnerships with other diversity-focused tech organizations, meet ups and training programs.

- Creating content that empowers speakers and attendees to share how they've successfully created diverse and inclusive environments. Focus on sharing solutions vs rant sessions about the state of diversity in the tech industry.

- Thoughtfulness around language used to promote activities, with attention paid to intersectionality. For example, do not list out all the possible URM groups you can think of in your marketing materials—website, social media pages, etc. You are bound to miss folks. Instead, let your audience know that your event/meetup is open and welcoming to everyone and discrimination will not be tolerated.

- Making people feel welcome through shirts in multiple sizes and cuts, pronoun stickers, and accessible, all-gender restrooms.

- Building out all spaces to make them accessible to all physical abilities, as well as including mother's rooms and prayer rooms.

- Ensuring social activities have a range of well-labeled food and drink options as well as activities for all interests and abilities.

The Best Practices

Now that we've reviewed the value of developer events, and what I've learned, I'll highlight a number of best practices that can be used to plan and execute high-value, measurable, inclusive experiences.

Know the audience

Whether it be through global developer research reports such as SlashData or bespoke projects, dive into the data. Have a strong foundation on the motivations, decision-making strategies, preferences and sentiments of your developer audience, and build the event narrative, strategy and plans around this knowledge.

Choose the right event strategy based on goals and resources

"Developer events" represents an extensive category of activities, from local meetups with tens or hundreds of attendees, up to marquee corporate events with tens of thousands.

Knowing that companies, organizations and teams will have varying goals, budgets and human resources, it's important to select the event type to match your objectives and constraints.

If your goal is to drive awareness and engagement in established gatherings of developers, then consider sponsoring relevant industry events, partner events, or trade shows.

Tips:

- Sponsorships can range from $1K for smaller events up to hundreds of thousands of dollars. In addition, most sponsorships will have an accompanying execution cost for things such as booth design and construction, swag, printing, and rentals. Depending on the number of staff needed, and the number of complimentary passes included in the sponsorship, you may also need to account for additional pass purchases. Budget in advance accordingly, and choose events selectively if your budget is limited.

- When prioritizing events, ask questions such as size and composition of the audience, whether your company has previously sponsored the event (and if so, if it was impactful), what post-event data will be provided as part of the sponsorship, whether the event aligns with key product announcements or stories, if it is minimally staffed, and if it has a code of conduct and commitment to diversity and inclusion.

- Aim for a sponsorship level that is commensurate with the size of your offering to the community. If you're new to the space, if your technology is not yet at parity with competitors, or if your offering hasn't changed from previous years, consider a presence that brings awareness and an opportunity to engage, but without overselling.

- Similarly, plan content that is appropriate for the stage the product or technology is in the adoption lifecycle, and that reinforces the availability of associated developer programs. For example, if people are not yet aware of your offering, focus on engaging lightning talks and demos, and have accompanying materials and swag branded with program information that reinforce how to learn more.

- If planning a physical presence, ensure the appropriate teams have committed to providing staff in advance. A good rule of thumb is to have a minimum of 2 technical staff per 10' x 10' space, and have them work half the show hours. So if a show floor is open for 8 hours a day, aim for a bare minimum of 4 technical staff total. Running labs or lightning talks in the space may require a slightly higher number. For events with a larger physical presence, also have an event manager on hand for space set up and troubleshooting. If an event manager is not available for all events, provide staff detailed instructions on setup, including onsite contacts for suppliers.

- If you're unable to guarantee the minimum number of staff, consider foregoing the physical space and select other items such as sponsored sessions, receptions or diversity lunches, which allow for engagement, but require fewer people to attend from your company.

- Ask in advance whether custom booth builds are allowed or required. If custom work is to be done, estimate workback time of at least 3 months. If not, adhere to the event's deadlines to avoid late fees and the suppliers running out of certain rental options.

If the goal is to reach communities where they're at, and at scale, then consider small sponsorships ($1K-$5K) for multiple events within a network of meetup groups (e.g. Google Developer group DevFests) or a series of topical events (e.g. DevOpsDays).

Tips:

- If budget and/or human resources are constrained, develop a "priority zero (P0)" and "priority one (P1)" list. Priority may be determined by criteria such as proximity to a company's office (and associated travel cost for staff/speakers), size of community, level of technical depth, how organized the community and its leadership are, whether there is a commitment to diversity. Commit to fund the P0, and if any events fall off the radar, and P1 events remain feasible, elevate.

- Ideally at least one person from the company should attend, whether it be a previous commitment through a selected paper, or to staff a small table. Having the brand represented on the site suggests a physical presence.

- "In-a-box" the physical presence with a tablecloth and pop-up banner, small and simple-yet-desired swag, such as stickers, and materials on relevant programs, which keeps the event on-brand, should add no more than a few hundred dollars to the cost, and is manageable for a single person to set up without an event manager.

- Measurement may be challenging, depending on how formal or informal the event. If attendee data is not part of the sponsorship, then use approximate swag distribution and online RSVPs (if public) as proxies for reach, and diligently document feedback captured via conversations. For the latter tactic, this may be accomplished through shared, collaborative docs or other internal bug tracking tools.

If the goal is to have a "tentpole" moment to focus press, analysts and customers, then consider a marquee company event or a product-specific conference.

Tips:

- Marquee events are big on budget and on human resources. Planning can take upwards of a year or more, especially to reserve ample space, select and onboard agencies, secure budget, and to get buy in from all necessary internal teams. You will need to work in particular with the product teams whose efforts will be highlighted, to ensure that the timing of the event properly aligns with release cycles and narratives.

- If the conferences will include regional editions, ensure that you document processes, content, demos, and project management trackers with reusability in mind so that regional marketing teams can execute independently. If it's not financially feasible to do regional events on one's own, consider extending the content and experiences through networks of developer communities.

If the goal is to build trust and credibility with strategic developers, then consider invitation-only summits.

Tips:

- High-touch summits at first glance are pricey for their size, although can deliver a high return-on-investment, so be thoughtful in who is invited, the exclusivity of the interactions and experiences, having any customer relationship tracking set up in advance, and ensuring that associated client teams (sales, partnerships, partner developer advocacy) are bought into the tracking and instructed on the processes.

Whatever your goal, an event is only as effective as its connection to a larger marketing plan and the post-event nurture strategy. Ensure that you're able to confidently answer questions such as:

- Are objectives clearly outlined, and can they be measured?

- Do the objectives ladder up to larger objectives around the product, technology or community?

- Do the tools and resources exist to follow up with leads, whether through client teams, email or both?

157

- Is there a post-event plan to "keep the lights on", such as a recap email, blog post series, event content amplification campaign (e.g. twice weekly tweets highlighting session recordings), or re-engagement via digital advertising?
- For the teams involved, does their post-event workload allow for the bandwidth to execute post-event activities?

If the resources do not exist to properly plan, staff and execute all phases of an event, including post-event, it's worth scaling back plans so that you are committed only to what you can fully deliver.

Map experiences back to well-known, well-established, highly valued developer programs

Events can be a conduit and focal point to promoting and accessing other developer programs. On the flip side, developer programs can provide substantial content and structure to the event's programming.

Do you have certification programs? Consider add-on trainings on day zero or after the event wraps for people to get certified. Request space at the event for people to come and ask questions and sign up for certification opportunities.

Do you provide hands-on labs? Create self-paced learning labs spaces on site. If you have the budget to provide equipment, consider doing so (especially if the output may need testing on mobile or Internet of Things devices). If not, "bring your own laptop" is OK, but should be well publicized both in advance and on site, and space and reliable Internet access are critical. For the latter, ensure that any account creation is simple, straightforward and doesn't involve a commitment to spend (such as entering a credit card).

Do you have budget for on-site video or podcast production? Develop a content strategy that not only creates content that developers can engage with virtually so as to feel part of the event, but is also informative and instructional outside the context of the event. Particularly for marquee events, there's such a concentration of company talent, try to make the most of this as budget and time allow. From a budget perspective, opting to do live streaming, session recording, onsite video creation (such as interviews), and potential upfront video production (such as videos for keynotes) may run in the upwards of hundreds of thousands of dollars for a multi-day, multi-track event.

Do you have ample space and staff? Build office hours, "birds of a feather," or app review sessions into the agenda as a way to provide discoverable access to experts and support resources. For office hours and app review sessions, pre-event registration may be worth considering (with the availability of a reliable activity registration system). However, if budget or tools do not allow for this, be sure to clearly communicate up front what the process will be for participating in such activities.

Don't leave goals and measurement until the end

Events should be purpose-driven, and choosing to do an event should automatically be associated with broader organizational goals (e.g. if, in Q2, one wishes to reach X Java developers, choosing to sponsor a particular event, and at a specific level, will help us reach a certain percentage of our goal).

From there, ensure that the tactics used have a way of being measured. This may include:

- Hosting labs or trainings, or delivering demos that can be tracked through analytics.

- Session and booth attendance data.

- Using social listening tools, such as Sysomos, Crimson Hexagon, or others vetted and approved by your company, to track reach, engagement and sentiment of specific social media conversations.

- Administering session-specific and post-event surveys, particularly when you're hosting the event (this may be more complex when sponsoring an event, depending on the host organization's policies on reaching out to their attendee list).

- Purchasing sponsorship elements that provide data, such as virtual bags and email marketing campaigns. Not only do they provide the upfront reach data, but when links are tagged, they can provide insight into actions taken from the clicks.

To document product feedback formally, it's critical to have an agreed collection method up front. This could be a shared collaboration document, internal bug tracking, or surveys administered as part of the space's experience. As a reminder, make sure you've adhered to your company's policies on survey administration in advance of the event.

Many of these methods are "upper funnel." By being diligent about creating analytics funnels and developer journeys, and using best practices around link tracking (whether it be through email marketing tools, UTM parameters in Google Analytics, or other digital measurement tools approved by your company), you can glean considerable useful information. For example: how many people have been reached, how they feel about the experience, what initial actions they take as a direct result of the event. From this you can deliver critical feedback to product organisations.

Have a good agency[2]

Depending on the size and type of event, and the available budget, some type of third-party agency support may be needed. This could include a digital shop to build a website, app or technical demos, or an event agency to build out the event space.

When reviewing agencies, consider factors such as:

- The shop's technical expertise (particularly for web, app and technical development).

- Their understanding of your company's brand, vision and the event's objectives.

- A clear sense of how they communicate on matters such as, timelines, documentation, budget, roles and responsibilities.

- Transparency around and agreement upon who will own the technology created (if applicable).

- If development will be done, adherence to your company's privacy and security requirements.

---

[2] also referred as 'shop'.

Budget ranges will vary substantially depending on the size and scope of the project (from tens of thousands to hundreds of thousands and beyond). Generally the cost of working with more experienced shops within the developer events and developer marketing space will be non-trivial (although they may also be more reliable partners). If budget is limited, prioritize using agencies for projects for which there is limited in-house expertise or bandwidth. For industry events and trade shows, limit custom booth design to the highest priority events; for others, consider investing in upfront asset design that can then be used for printing on brand backdrops for turn-key booths.

Choose desirable swag

Swag ('Stuff We All Get') can be used at events to raise awareness (placing company or program brand on a permanent object), sentiment (delight in receiving a gift), and engagement (an invitation to approach a staff member or an incentive to participate in an activity). Thoughtful, useful and unique items are valued by recipients. We've all seen queues on the expo floor for limited edition t-shirts, socks or plushies, or crowds for a device raffle, and to a degree, these are expected. Delightful items can help inspire your next brand ambassador. It's important that items are of reasonable quality and utility, and reflect the event organizer's understanding of the audience. My best source of ideas has come from within the Developer Relations team, and asking others what they see and receive at events.

Here are best practices for planning swag for events:

- Partner with reliable vendors, and understand what they do and do not provide (e.g. design, storage, shipping/logistics).

- Plan upfront as much as possible (order in bulk to save on costs).

- Understand internal brand approval processes, and ensure that logo usage is consistent with brand guidelines.

- Request samples, ideally with your company's brand so you can confirm that the vendor used the specs properly. Place samples in a public space to gather feedback from your team.

- Avoid gender-specific items, and if ordering clothing, select multiple cuts and a full range of sizes.

- Think through storage (Do you have enough on site? Can the vendor store?) and confirm an inventory management solution.

- Understand customs requirements and tracking methods, as well as what you're responsible for and what the vendor is managing.

- If the swag is something not available in all markets, work with the appropriate internal teams on approvals, communications and alternative items.

- Know the rules around giving items to government employees and other compliance issues.

- If the item is associated with a contest or raffle, follow your company's procedures around competitions (and plan well in advance for cycles of approvals).

Don't forget the details

In the end, it's often the little things that get overlooked and cause the biggest headaches. Here's a checklist of questions to ask for each event, knowing that depending on size and scope, they may not all be applicable, or may be owned by others (making it your role to confirm that the work is attended to):

- Do all relevant teams know your plans?

- Is there ample staffing from the right areas of expertise?

- Have all items from the sponsorship checklist been submitted?

- Have all rentals (AV, furniture) been placed by the deadline?

- Has any company-provided technology (e.g. laptops, tablets) been reserved?

- Has the right level of Internet connectivity been ordered?

- Has new content been prepared if needed?

- Have print orders been placed?

- Has swag been ordered?

- Have any legal or PR requests been submitted?
- Have deliveries been sent to arrive by the correct receiving deadlines?
- Have you created a "know before you go" to inform staff of the event plans?
- Has catering been ordered?
- Is there a social media strategy? Or a media strategy of any kind (video, photography, etc...)?

Get event experience

The beauty and challenge of managing developer events is that the best way to learn is through hands-on experience. If you are new to the practice of developer marketing or developer events planning, find opportunities to attend others' events, simply to listen, observe, and engage with attendees. Inquire within your company as to whether they'll allow you to attend a certain number of events each year for professional development (and if they'll fund your attendance). Join a local meetup group. Seek out internal projects for your company's developer events. Stay informed on the latest trends and sentiment by following influencers within developer communities on social media and by paying close attention to their thoughts on the events in which they participate.

Document what you learn, and incorporate the best of what you observe into your own common practices.

Balance innovation and opportunity

Technology companies are constantly pushing the boundaries of what's possible, and have the capacity to inspire developers to create game-changing applications and businesses with cutting edge tools and products. However, for many smaller companies, seeing examples of what larger companies have built may be aspirational, but not actionable.

Inspiration succeeds when it has an eye towards opportunity for the developer. Is the technology stable? Are there communities and resources available? Will this help to grow productivity, relevance in the job market, recognition, and success? These are the questions you need to answer to encourage attendees to engage and help them get the most from the experience.

Events, the programs they promote and resources they generate (such as labs, video content, follow up emails, and extended series of meetups), present focused opportunities. They can tell stories by building brand awareness and positive sentiment, and also drive momentum around other impactful developer tools and programs.

Conclusion

This guide is not exhaustive, and doesn't go into great detail around timelines, trackers, budgeting, creative briefs, or how to work effectively with cross-functional partners. What this guide represents is tips, best practices and perspectives gathered through personal experiences. If I leave you with anything, I hope it is that:

- Events can yield a strong return-on-investment, particularly when closely aligned with other highly-valued developer programs.

- Although developers "cannot be marketed to," there are ways to create magic moments, especially if you focus on trustworthy, authentic, deeply technical experiences.

- With thoughtfulness and upfront planning, diversity, inclusion and accessibility can be interwoven into the event, increasing satisfaction, trust and respect.

- It is important that you don't underestimate the importance of budget and human resources in planning and executing events, including the post-event work cycle.

Good luck, have fun, and deliver impact!

Chapter 11 | Developing The Right Mindset To Create Great Content

Matthew Pruitt: Head of Global Community & Social Media - Unity

This chapter will take you through real-life examples and best practices, as well as help you create the best possible content. Throughout, you will learn the importance of process and how critical it is to clearly convey it to everyone you work with. Building great content requires buy-in from an entire team, big or small, and you'll walk away from this chapter outfitted with some helpful tips and data to make that happen.

Introduction

To bring attention to your project, you need highly engaging content. People only remember 20% of what they've read online if there is no accompanying visual (https://sdata.me/UsSKAT). With all of the content that is on the internet at any given moment, yours needs to stand out.

You might think this means that there's a lot of hard work in your future, but that's not true. Engaging content doesn't need to be insanely complicated, luxurious, or expensive to create. Remember what you were told as a kid: keep it simple, stupid.

Stop for a second and think about the content you see when scrolling through Facebook. Those videos with a ton of shares and likes are likely cats doing funny things. I'm not telling you to put cats in your content (or am I?), but you get the point. Highly engaging content is something that quickly and effectively catches your viewers' eyes and draws them in.

I am the Head of Global Community & Social Media at Unity Technologies. My team and I oversee all social media marketing and community campaigns across the company. Before joining Unity Technologies, I spent time in multiple marketing and product roles at IGN Entertainment, Machinima, Electronic Arts, and Quicken Loans. In my previous roles I worked across multiple business disciplines including product management, product marketing, and online marketing. Having operated in both the product and marketing ecosystems, I've been able to draw valuable insights that have helped me bridge gaps in organizational communication.

When I started at Unity two years ago, content was like gold: it was sparse, but when you found it, it was priceless. To try and create awesome social media posts that are engaging and interesting to our audience without compelling content is tough, to say the least. My team and I had two choices: accept it for what it was and keep trudging on, or do something to change it. We chose the latter. And if you're in a similar scenario, you should too.

The path to great content is earned

Unity is not a small company, it employs over 1,500 people. Those 1,500 plus people are working on making amazing demos, editorial improvements, tutorials, educational articles, and so much more. And by the way, they are also pumping out a lot of content as part of their day jobs. Content is good. Engaging content is great. There's a very big difference there that is extremely important to understand. If you're developing as part of a team or on your own, you owe it to yourself and/or your team to create GREAT content. Why would you want anything less? Only the best should be representing your project or product.

So my team and I took a "road trip" of sorts. We started to meet with every team within Unity that touches content and go through best-in-class examples of great, engaging content. But we didn't just show them great content and say "do this," we built a meaningful relationship and educated them on the WHY. Explaining the process is more critical than the outcome. In general, I think it's safe to say that employees, and people in general, don't want to be told what to do. Rather, they want to be empowered with valuable information to make informed decisions.

For example, we met with our Evangelism team, who create amazing Unity video tutorials for the developer community. They were uploading tutorial videos weekly on our YouTube channel and, while they performed well, my team knew they could perform better with one major tweak - duration - to make the transformation from good content to great content.

Data shows that users consume content, especially video content, in short chunks. A 60-minute video tutorial would not be classified as a "short chunk." We suggested to the Evangelism team that they break down their 60 minute tutorial videos into shorter, bite-sized chunks of about three to five minutes. The team pushed back against this change in methodology as it would take them a little more time to cut up the segments and just weren't sold that it would be worth their time.

You will experience push-backs when trying to create change, but remember that this is a good thing! This opens the door for you to educate through data and build a stronger relationship. This is a natural occurrence at any company, big or small, so keep cool and carry on.

Our response to the Evangelism team was that we totally understood their hesitation, but let's test it. They agreed that the next few tutorial videos they published would be broken into smaller chunks and we would measure performance against the long-form videos. This is exactly the outcome that we wanted. They were joining us on the journey and we would discover the answer together.

The results spoke for themselves. During the test, we saw a 49% increase in total views and a 239% increase in average percent viewed - meaning that people were watching more. Smaller, bite-sized segments allow users to find what they're looking for much more quickly and allow them to easily pick back up where they left off.

Sure, it would have saved time and been easier if they would have just listened to us in the first place, but that likely would have led to more conversations down the road and required even more time because people tend to fall back into what is familiar if they don't experience the learning process first-hand. That's exactly why I said that the process is more critical than the outcome. They are now empowered with the knowledge to create engaging content. And they know why they're doing it!

Now that I've walked you through one example of how to turn good content in to great content, I want to dive deeper into the content itself, best practices, and where and how to deploy it.

Mindset makes great content

We've already discussed that it's important to build relationships and educate on your thought process to deliver great content. But the mindset needed to create great content isn't just communication and education, it is also needed if you are working individually. You don't need to work in a large organization or have multiple teams to support you. I've seen great, successful content produced by solo indie developers and that's because they put themselves in the right mindset.

Let's explore what I mean by developing the right mindset. Before you start creating content, you should be asking yourself two very important questions: "What is the one takeaway I want someone to have after viewing my content?" And "Why should they care?"

Think back to the beginning of this chapter when I said "keep it simple, stupid." Ask yourself those two very questions and you're already miles ahead of your competitors.

Everything you do should be viewed through the lens of your end users. Sometimes we get too close to our project and we forget why our end user should or would care. By asking yourself those two questions, it forces you to take a step back and look at your project objectively and then allows for your content to reflect that. That doesn't mean that we don't want users to connect to the material - we absolutely do. But you want them to be able to form their own opinion through a clearly communicated message.

A great example of this is posting on social media for the sake of posting on social media. Sometimes my team gets requests to post that someone from Unity will be speaking at an event. Don't get me wrong, that's important and exciting, but why would our end user care? Unless they're attending the event, there is no relevance to the greater audience. This doesn't mean we don't post about it at all, it just means that we need to work harder to make it more engaging by asking questions such as "Is it being live streamed?", "What are the topics they're talking about?", "Are there any new announcements?" These questions are allowing us the opportunity to potentially build an exciting piece of engaging content.

If you take one thing away from this, remember the fact that we don't know what we don't know. You don't want a potential user to make assumptions about your project. They don't know what you know - they didn't work on the project. Like any good story, you want to take them on a journey that paints the full picture of what your project is and for them to walk away wanting a sequel. In this case, the sequel is playing your game, watching your movie, using your product, or whatever it may be.

Video is THE MOST engaging piece of content that you can create for your project. It's no coincidence that Facebook's algorithms place a higher value on video than static graphics or text. They know that videos generate more views, more engagement, and lead to higher conversion, whether it's a purchase or simply a click to a website to learn more. And did you know that YouTube is the second largest search engine behind Google? Video is key. That said, video is also the most complicated asset (in terms of time and effort) to create. While I can't stress enough how important video is, don't think that it's the be all end all of ways to market your project. If you're in a larger organization, high-quality video is probably more possible to obtain than if you're a one-person team. And that's OK, because now that you're in the right mindset to develop great content, your possibilities are limitless.

Sometimes all you have to work with are static images. Static images are the least ideal asset to have because they don't stand out. That doesn't mean that static images can't be valuable, but they're more of a complimentary piece. Once you get your user into the consumer journey funnel, static assets are a good way to give them more information and keep them wanting more. But as I've said before, there's good content and great content.

However, here's one solution. Let's say you're in a room of 15 statues. You're staring at all of them and all of the sudden one of them moves. Your eyes will immediately focus on that and everything else gets blurred out. It's human nature. Static assets work the exact same way. There's a great app called "Lumyer" that I absolutely love. It gives you the ability to add elements of motion to still images. All of the elements are pre-created so the time and effort spent by you is minimal. There are all kinds of different apps and programs that do this, but this is a simple example of how to transform your static image from good to great and ensure that it stands out above the rest.

I was recently at a social media conference where an agency used Lumyer to turn a client's static image into a motion graphic. The company created candles and were posting still images of their candles on their Facebook page. The agency came in, added a flicker motion to the flame of the candles and their purchase conversion increased by 250%. Five minutes of effort for a massive increase.

Make your content work harder for you. I've been a part of many conversations over the years where I hear "Oh, we don't have any content." 95% of the time, that has not been the case. Sometimes it takes getting creative with what you do have. Get scrappy and start digging through all of the raw assets available to you. I promise that there will be something that you can transform into engaging content.

As long as you're developing the right mindset along the way, content will come more easily. Much like the education process that was discussed earlier, focus more on the journey than the end result. If you're setting yourself up correctly from the beginning, the end result will usually take care of itself.

In terms of asset importance, remember that video reigns supreme, followed by motion graphics and still graphics in that order. They all have their place in the marketing food chain to communicate different messages. So now that we've established what great content looks like, the next section will dive into where, why, and how to deploy those assets so that you're maximizing their value.

Deploying content in social media: best practices

The Internet is a big place full of many people and many places. Now that you've created some awesome assets, you need to get the attention of the right people in the right places. Like any good salesperson, you need to go to them where they live, not the other way around. Luckily there is something called social media that makes this task a whole lot easier.

For the sake of this section, we're going to focus on three main social media channels: Facebook, Twitter, and YouTube. If you have to pick three to market your project, it should be them. Facebook is an awesome tool for shareability, Twitter allows you to be a part of multiple conversations through hashtags and tagging, and YouTube is the second largest search engine behind Google.

This is not a deep dive into every social media tool, this is meant to lightly touch on the best practices for each and to point you in the right direction. There are a ton of social media books in the marketplace and I highly suggest reading some of them. Just like the assets you created, you want to ensure that these tools are working the hardest for you.

Facebook

As we find at Unity, and as you'll probably find for your project, Facebook is not generally where your core audience lives, and that's OK! Facebook tends to be comprised of a more vast, general audience that loves great content, but it may not translate to an end user. This doesn't mean that it's any less valuable, in fact, it makes it more valuable to the realm of brand awareness, which is Facebook's strength. Play to the strengths of each social media tool and you'll have all of your bases covered.

Be sure to create your Facebook page as a business page. While Facebook posts don't populate in search engines, it's one of the best ways for your content to get shared. Populate your page with all of the relevant information and assets before pushing it live. Once live, this is when you need to start being a marketer.

If you're a one-person or small team, be sure to have all of your friends like your page and share your content. Sharing on Facebook is the fastest way to bring attention to your content and grow your page. Your friends are an easy access point into jump starting that process, so ask them to help out. If you're part of a larger organization, use your company's employees! This is so important and something that I can't stress enough. If you receive any push back from employees who are wary of using their own personal social media, be sure to highlight examples of positive reactions from the community to previous social media posts and explain the important of shareability and spreading the word. It might take some time, but they'll see the light.

Employees are the best evangelists for your project or product. At Unity, I send out weekly "Social Shareable" emails to the entire company, including our C-Suite. In that email, I highlight the best performing social content that we've posted and use easy one-click share buttons that allows them to share it on their personal Facebook pages. Not only does this give great visibility to the entire company on how social media is performing, but it also includes them as part of the process.

This is the next stage of developing the right mindset. You've used the process to create great content, now you need to evolve it to evangelize your team or organization to act on your behalf. Inclusion is one of the best ways to do that. Be sure to explain to them why it's important they help support your social initiatives. Again, it's about the journey more than the end result.

As we discussed previously, Facebook's algorithms favor video assets. So if you have video, this is the place to use it. Be sure that you're uploading it natively versus linking to YouTube or somewhere else. Native video is prioritized the highest by Facebook, so ensure that you're taking advantage of every extra inch you can.

If you're part of a larger organization or have a little bit of money to spare, you can boost some of your posts. Facebook has a massive, in-depth segmentation library for you to choose from. You can ensure that your money works the hardest for you by choosing locations, audiences, and/or interests that most pertain to your content. This is also a great way to help build your Facebook audience. By delivering them relatable content, you're now able to reach an entirely new set of people that you likely wouldn't be able to reach with organic social media.

Twitter

As much as Facebook is about brand awareness and reach, Twitter is about connecting with your users on a more 1:1 basis. At Unity, we find that the majority of our most leaned-in, core users live on Twitter. This provides us an excellent opportunity to ensure that the content and messaging we put out on Twitter is most relevant to those users.

The ability for a user to directly tweet you and engage in a 1:1 conversation is invaluable. It allows you to build interest and engagement on a micro level, while at the same time covering the macro as well. Use Twitter as a tool to push out content, but also ensure that you're maximizing its capability to connect with users. As an example, while our Unity Twitter is not a customer support account, we do have direct messages come to us from users who may be experiencing issues with billing or their account. We're always happy to connect them with a customer support representative directly via email rather than letting their message sit there unreplied to.

At Unity, our best performing tweets (measured by engagement - shares, likes, retweets, replies) are those that are generally technical in nature, such as a new editor feature release. These posts always enjoy the most engagement, but it doesn't mean that we don't support them with engaging assets. GIFs are very popular on Twitter and get shared widely. Sometimes if we have a video that has a really cool, engaging sequence within it, we'll pull it out and create a GIF that we'll then share separately on Twitter. This is a quick and easy way to expand the life of an asset and create a format that is more likely to be shared wider.

There are many tools out there that allow you to do this, including YouTube's own integrated tool. It's yet another simple tip that allows you to take good content and make it great for the vehicle in which it's living. You may have heard the saying "The right message in the right place at that right time." This is an example of that. Recognize who your user is, where they're living, and how they like to consume content.

Another fantastic feature of Twitter is the use of hashtags. You may see some people that create a tweet and have about 30 hashtags after it - don't be that person. Hashtags are actually very important and allow you to enter wider conversations without having to already have an established audience. For example, at Unity, our most popular hashtags are #unity3d, #gamedev, and #indiedev.

These hashtags pool together all of the conversations that are using them across Twitter. So, obviously, you want to ensure that you're using relevant hashtags. Find hashtags that are relevant to your project and include them in your tweet. Be sure to limit them to two or three per tweet, otherwise it just looks like spam. And there's no faster way to kill your content than people thinking it's spam. Stay brief and to the point in all of your social media postings - less is always more. Remember that, in most instances, your social media post's goal is to drive someone to do something (click, watch, learn more, etc.).

So now that you're ready to create your tweet, I'll leave you with a few final thoughts. As with anything, make sure you have a great, engaging asset. Make sure that you're using hashtags. And most importantly, make sure you're creating a "what's next." Meaning, be sure that you're directing them somewhere, whether it's to your website, blog, or another page. You want to keep your users in the consumer journey funnel so that they can learn more. Twitter is the top of the funnel, be sure that you're helping them stay and get to the bottom.

YouTube

The last social media property I'll touch on is YouTube. Did I already tell you it's the second largest search engine behind Google? That's a rhetorical question, but I say it again because it's just so important. Even if you only have one or two videos currently, create a YouTube page for your project and upload them!

If you're running a website or blog for your project and you want to place videos on those pages, be sure you're using the YouTube video embed. Embedding the video with YouTube versus other websites allows you to gain their SEO advantage and also keep your users within one ecosystem.

As previously mentioned with the Unity training tutorial videos, video length is very important. Try to keep your videos to two to three minutes and make sure you're jumping into the "what" as soon as possible. Most people only watch three to five seconds of a video before they decide whether they're staying or leaving. You must grab their attention in this timespan if you want your content to be successful.

Video titles are almost as important as the video content itself. Make sure that you're putting a lot of thought into your title before publishing. Try to include your company name, project name, and a brief description of what the video is. If your video is a trailer, make sure you're actually saying "trailer" in the title. Trailers are hugely popular and a frequent search term on

YouTube, so you want to ensure that you're part of that search criteria if someone searches it.

YouTube video descriptions are also very important. This is a text based field that allows you to write a quick description of what the video is and why they should care. It also allows you the opportunity to insert links to your other social media properties and websites. Use this space because if someone really loves your content, they're going to want to learn more. And if you don't make that readily available to them, they're not going to try and hunt it down.

The final aspect of YouTube I'll touch on is the use of an end screen. An end screen is a native feature of YouTube that allows you to include interactive elements at the end of your video such as a link to another video, link to your website, or a subscribe button. These are all meant to help keep the viewer in the funnel, so take advantage of them!

Next steps

We covered a lot in this chapter and I want to take the opportunity to pause and reflect. This chapter started with the idea of developing a mindset for both a team and yourself. If everyone is on the same page, it makes it a lot easier to execute great content. If you really take this seriously and make it an objective, you will find success.

If there's one thing you do right now after reading this chapter, go talk to your teams and build relationships. If you're a small team, start looking at the assets you already have and start thinking about how they can work harder for you. Great content, much like a great plan, is built over time. Don't rush it. Build it organically and ensure that everyone is following along the way.

Remember to have fun. Your content and your assets should reflect the joy that goes into your project. You want to make sure that's visible to your users. Stop and think about the message you want to convey and, with that in mind, look objectively at the assets available to you and how you can convert them from good to great.

I also highly suggest reading literature on overall marketing, content and social media. There are a ton of books out there, so I won't list them, but continue to educate yourself. As much as I talked about educating others on the process, you should be doing the same for yourself. Never stop learning.

Also, when you're surfing the Internet and a great piece of content catches your eye, stop and note the thing that made you care about it. Why did you stop scrolling to watch? Did you click for more info? Why? Ask yourself these questions and apply what your answer is to your own project strategy.

Creating engaging content isn't hard if you set yourself up for success from the very beginning. Good luck and start creating!

Chapter 12 | Closing Thoughts: How To Attract, Engage And Retain Developers

Stephen Donnelly: Technology Lead, Software & Platform Industry Group - Accenture

Introduction

We have covered a lot of ground in this book, ranging from the creation of developer personas and the importance of community, to how to run events, how to connect experts with developers, how to nurture hardware developers, and how to find great content - and the right mindset - for developer marketing. This, in itself, shows the broad scope a developer program covers.

There have been common themes throughout the book such as the increasing influence of developers, and how they dislike traditional marketing and, instead, refer to each other for positive opinion before making a technology selection. The authors have explained how to understand the dynamics of developer communities. They have explained the need to tread lightly, because skilful developer marketing is about two-way feedback: allowing you to present authentic information and receive valuable product feedback. The preceding chapters have provided some extraordinary insights from those who have worked in developer marketing as it comes of age.

To round off this book, in this chapter we explore some of those common themes, and discuss some new insights in an interview with a seasoned professional of the developer marketing industry, Stephen Donnelly, from Accenture's Software & Platform Industry Group.

Stephen, please can you tell us a little about your current role and your experience in developer marketing and building developer ecosystems?

I am the Technology Lead for Accenture's Software & Platform Industry group and the global lead for Developer Ecosystem Services, based out of Accenture's San Francisco office. Within this role I provide the technology strategy and vision for the group and act as the technical lead for a number of global development teams. Accenture's Software & Platforms Industry recognizes that, by the very precise nature of being 'born digital', leading companies have interrupted business for incumbent industries such as media, communications, and retail, enabling the meteoric rise of the most valuable companies on earth. Platform companies lead with technology, often owning the full digital experience from device through to cloud-based services. We define a developer ecosystem as a system of interconnected elements that developers engage with to build products and services on top of platforms. I consider developers to represent the heartbeat of digital innovation, making a thriving developer ecosystem critically important to the success of any platform or technology.

Many companies have traditionally equated managing a developer ecosystem with exposing a set of APIs, coupling this technology with static knowledge base content and providing some level of developer support. However, this isn't sufficient in today's dynamic landscape. When thinking of a developer ecosystem as a system of interconnected elements enabling developers to build products and services on top of an existing platform, it helps to view this as a living entity with constantly evolving needs. The most innovative and fastest growing companies in the world nurture their developer ecosystem through a comprehensive approach that incorporates content, marketing and support.

Throughout this book, we have seen two themes emerge:

- *developer influence is increasingly felt throughout organizations, even those that are not traditionally thought to be "software" companies*

- *developers are "marketing averse"*

Does your experience tally with what we've been reporting? How and why have things changed over the last 5 years?

Yes, I absolutely agree. At Accenture, I have noticed the changing nature of client conversations within the last five years. Conversations that predominantly dealt with operational aspects of developer support - how to scale efficiently, how to maximize throughput, how to minimize average handling time - have evolved into more strategic questions. "Can you help me identify, segment and connect with my developer audience?", "Should I embrace open-source?", "Should I allow third-party developers to have self-service access?"

It is not only the nature of conversations that have changed. The developer landscape has shifted significantly over the last five years. Developers are growing in numbers and importance. Their skills and capabilities are highly prized, and competition for developer mindshare is rapidly intensifying. Their work leads to revenue growth, higher market valuation and helps to ensure the continued relevance of the company. Developers are becoming more influential within organizations as engineers hold c-suite positions, and they increasingly carry organizational weight, influencing a large percentage of a company's technology spend upon toolsets, software and storage. An interesting observation, that has struck me within the last year or more, is that developers are increasingly evaluating developer ecosystem capabilities when selecting vendors - they are appraising more than simply the technical capabilities of the product or service and are evaluating the API suite, documentation, integration partner landscape and support structure. Developers are key decision-makers when determining whether it is hype or reality. A vibrant developer ecosystem can prove to be a differentiating factor for many of the companies that we work with.

The technology landscape also continues to change at pace. With the advent of the Internet - particularly the emergence of the cloud, open-source and vastly reduced costs for storage, hardware and processing power - developers have emerged from the shadows into the light. Recent advances toward API-centric and microservices architecture and programmable infrastructure have expanded developers' potential exponentially over the last five years. Technology powers the value propositions, compelling use cases, competitive advantages and unique selling propositions of almost every breakout client that we have worked with in this period. It is a small step to view developers as authors of coded innovation and pioneers of the art of the possible.

As the industry becomes more congested, as barriers to entry continue to lower, and with developers being able to more easily move across platforms, there's little room for companies to assume that the strength of their technology alone will attract and retain developers. Those responsible for developer ecosystems need to understand what developers think of their ecosystem, determine where its capabilities stand relative to peers and define the actions that will help them move toward differentiation and best-in-class. This must be done in lock-step with their developer base - catering to the needs of this evolving set of stakeholders is fundamental to success.

As organizations work to advance their developer ecosystems, marketing is a critical tool in the tool box, but not the only one. Developers can certainly be marketing averse - at least as it relates to traditional marketing approaches. They are a savvy bunch. They know when someone's trying to sell to them and it can be negatively received, causing an almost visceral response. I've been at developer conferences within the last few years where you can sense a shift in the mood in the room, almost imperceptibly, when a Sales / Marketing professional takes to the stage - often before he or she says a single word.

Understanding the people element of developer marketing is key to doing it well. If you set your KPIs around operations ("What's the efficiency?", "What is the throughput?", "What is the average handling time?") and ignore the experience, your developers will sense that the support they're receiving is purely transactional. Empathetic support is very important, because developers value that you care about resolving the problem. You need to focus your KPIs around the developer experience and the quality of the support. A good example is that you should not mandate a strict time component to resolving a developer's issue. The developer shouldn't feel like you're trying to get them out of the chat window or off the phone, and the support engineer needs to be able to focus on one issue at a time, so there isn't a delay or the sense that the issue is one of many.

Building a strong developer experience is directly analogous, but not identical, to building customer satisfaction: good content and strong support are key and KPIs should center on these elements. There are, of course, a number of key challenges inherent in measuring developer satisfaction: some options to try are using the Net Promoter Score, social sentiment analysis and developer surveys to determine whether your product or service is being well received by developers. I work with companies who are also experimenting with Developer Satisfaction Score (DSAT). However, it's not straightforward to establish this information, or to extrapolate to determine future targets to work upon.

One challenge is that almost all of these methods for measuring satisfaction were set up for customers and do not appreciate the subtle, nuanced, differing needs that developers have. Another challenge is that a lot of what needs to be measured is intangible and difficult to quantify. As an example, I know that the developer experience is highly important. I also know that the network effect of developers is very meaningful. I don't yet have empirical data to back either of those assumptions. A final, interesting challenge which feels like it belongs with the developer experience, is inspiration - how do you inspire developers? It almost becomes an existential question, touching on many areas; aspiration, autonomy, future, growth, impact, meaning, purpose, recognition, reward, sustainability... For me, it's an intriguing challenge that we are keen to crack, and I anticipate this to be a very interesting area of growth.

As you consider the developer experience, focus on what developers value. Accenture research shows that developers don't prize a slick layout of materials, dazzling developer events or collectible swag as highly as accurate content and timely support. They are very pragmatic; they appreciate value and usefulness. The key, therefore, when targeting developers, is to focus on value and to ensure that your messaging consistently reflects this. There are a number of questions to ask yourself when determining value, for example:

- What is the value that your company offers to developers?

- Is that value relevant to developers today?
- Will it continue to be relevant?
- What use cases does your product, service or platform satisfy?
- How does your offering compare with that of your competitors?
- Do you make the developer's life better, or their job easier?
- What do developers' peers think of your platform, product or service?
- Will the time that developers invest in learning how to develop on your platform be valuable to them in the future?
- Do you enable developers to solve problems that they find challenging? Will the developer continue to be challenged over time?
- Do you offer developers the tools or training with which developers can master your technology?

In this context, marketing takes on a broader definition. It is about engaging developers by demonstrating value and a market position that is uniquely attractive. It is about providing education, challenging developers and giving them the ability to learn and to master, and offering the content and services really needed by the developer groups that are most attractive to the organization.

How do you reconcile the twin themes we've just discussed to make your developer marketing effective?

With developers becoming perhaps the most critical stakeholder group that platform companies serve, developer engagement is simply essential. But this is a much more comprehensive challenge than just marketing. Research that Accenture has carried out within 2018[3] indicates that companies have many

---

[3] ABOUT ACCENTURE DEVELOPER ECOSYSTEM RESEARCH

The Accenture Developer Ecosystem Research study is based on a survey conducted online in December 2017 with over 750 software developers based in the U.S. The opportunities to improve the ways in which they engage, support and target the developer community. An emphasis on improving content, education and support is required. There is still significant opportunity for savvy companies to become a preferred platform for development. What might have been perceived as offering a competitive advantage five years ago has now become a strategic necessity. The game isn't over, but action is needed now.

When marketing to, and interacting with, developers, honesty and respect are key. This becomes particularly relevant when working with key influencers. If you try anything that's not legitimate, they will know it and they will share it. Whether you're addressing known issues, changing your infrastructure, updating code fixes, considering new features, or releasing new products or services, being open and honest about your plans is very important. Developers respond favorably to being treated as a valued stakeholder. They do not respond favorably to being commoditized.

For example, if you're building something that has a particular feature, and you're writing copy to reflect that, everything needs to be actually true. Developers will read it and try it out - although they don't like to admit it (and I include myself here!), developers are very strong at testing and will find the issues that exist with your product or service. In addition, highly engaged developer communities, social media channels and sites like Stack Overflow up the ante by giving disillusioned developers the platforms to voice their anger or frustration. You have to be honest and transparent or developers will call you out.

Being clear and direct are also highly valued by the developer set. In developer marketing you have to be crystal clear. It's almost like you need to speak a unique language, complete with its own tone and cadence, and there is a different way of writing when addressing a developer audience. Developers respond favourably to content that has been written by developers, and

---

respondents were at least 18 years old, self-identified as software developers and/or program as a hobby, or contributed to open source projects and had been programming for at least one year, spending a minimum of 10 hours per week coding. The respondents represented a combination of public and private companies and organizations of varying size. The survey and related data analysis quantifies perceptions of various platforms' developer ecosystems, likelihood of recommending those platforms, and preferences for interacting with developer ecosystems. In a separate study, Accenture also surveyed over 1000 developers in China in May 2018.

like content that gives them exactly what they need, nothing superfluous. This can be an interesting challenge when you have a diverse developer base, and further highlights the importance of knowing your developers intimately, especially those who you have identified as influencers. Not only should you engage them as directly as possible in order to get their specific inputs and guidance, but you should also view them as a proxy for the developer audience that you are trying to engage with.

I have worked with companies who invite key influencers to their head office once a year to participate in a design sprint, to view early product prototypes or to discuss the upcoming year's product backlog. Other companies give influencers advance access to software/product releases, give them special status at key events or invite them to speak at, and participate in, internal company events. I have also witnessed companies who set up the equivalent of a steering committee populated by third party developers (an influencer panel if you will). Closing the distance between your company and your developer base not only gives you great insights into how your product/service is being used and tremendously valuable future requirements; it also allows the influencers (and their networks by extension) to feel a greater sense of ownership and buy-in by being able to directly shape the future offerings of the companies that they love.

Without wanting to open a 'Software Developer" vs. "Software Engineer" debate here, I like to think of developers as engineers. Engineers are problem solvers. They value things that are inherently useful, which can include marketing if it's actually helpful. They are naturally curious - and will be interested in stuff that teaches them something rather than promotes something to buy. They like to be challenged. Can your product or service allow them to solve a challenging problem in an interesting way? And, once you have piqued their interest in the challenge, do you provide them the tools, channels, content and support to master it? For this reason, marketing initiatives that include tutorials, lunch-and-learns, and so forth can be a good fit for this audience. Once the challenge has been accepted, then mastered, influencers will often contribute back to the community, not only sharing their knowledge and experience but actively helping fellow developers on their journey.

Finally, as I mentioned earlier, the crux of good developer engagement is to always focus on value. In the context of marketing, activities offer value by promoting insights on the latest technology. Present your platform, product or service as an enabler and demonstrate the opportunities that it can offer to your developers. How you represent yourself when positioning emerging technology presents a strong opportunity to demonstrate thought leadership. This is key to showing that you are forward-thinking, that you have an opinion on what is happening with the latest technology, that you know how this might affect your product or service, that you have a view on where you see the industry going and why, and that you are aware how that may impact the developers with whom you engage. Thought leadership is an attribute that is highly regarded by developers, particularly those that work within technology in developing countries.

Where should a team invest its developer marketing and support dollars to have the most impact? How important do you think it is to use survey data to establish where to spend?

How a team should invest its developer marketing and support dollars is strongly linked back to the segmentation that you will have done - who are your target developer groups and what do these target developer groups tell you that they want and need? The developer ecosystem may include company employees, large and small partners, full-time independent developers and a range of part-time developers across many geographies. Their wants and needs vary greatly but are specific and highly nuanced. Once the 'who' has been established, you can then consider the 'what' and the 'how'.

For example, in the 2018 Accenture Developer Ecosystem Survey we learned that nearly three-quarters of US survey respondents want to learn new skills, or improve current skills, when engaging with a developer ecosystem. We also discovered that learning is of particular value to professional developers and to those working in medium-sized organizations and enterprises. It does not come as a complete surprise to recognize that learning is at the forefront of developer needs. The technologies and techniques of software development advance at a breakneck pace and being skilled in the latest and greatest is often the key to being valued. Developers are also highly motivated by peer acknowledgement and they share their learning openly. Whilst it's intuitive that developers want to learn new skills, a surprising finding from our study was how large the opportunity is for companies to improve their learning capabilities and cater to this pressing developer need.

Additionally, Accenture's China Developer Ecosystem Survey found that developers in China express a broader spectrum of needs than those based in the US, with 80% of survey respondents agreeing that a company's developer ecosystem is critically important to them. Chinese developers have many different expectations from the platforms they use, with the most important being that the ecosystem helps them to solve interesting problems in a creative way; it helps them provide more value to clients; and they are able to learn new skills or improve current skills when engaging with the developer ecosystem. With only a minority of Chinese developers being fluent in English, almost three-quarters said that it was important that platforms provide developer notes in their native language - an important consideration for any platform wanting to attract those developers.

So, understanding the nuanced needs of your developer ecosystem segments provides critical insights into where and how to invest. For me, the three main areas of a vibrant developer ecosystem are **content**, **support** and **marketing**, with all three being strongly interconnected.

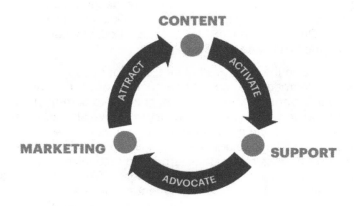

Content can make or break a developer ecosystem. It has to be written for the developer audience without spin or marketing gloss, get straight to the point, and have an uncomplicated design. Establishing a comprehensive content strategy typically requires a multi-faceted approach, encapsulating developer notes, quick-start guides, case studies, code samples, whitepapers, blogs and tutorials. Documentation on APIs and SDKs needs to be comprehensive and up-to-date. Content delivery is equally critical. Content needs to be available where developers digitally live - in example areas such as developer forums and social media.

In Accenture's 2018 Developer Ecosystem research, technically accurate and up-to-date content ranked as the two most important elements in a company's developer ecosystem of the 15 elements the research queried - again, indicative of the pragmatic nature of this community. More experienced developers rate content's importance higher than less experienced developers. And "workhorses" (professional developers who program more than 50 hours per week) rate the importance of all aspects of content (accuracy, currency, findability, consistency, readability) higher than those who program fewer hours per week.

Support is necessary in a variety of ways across multiple channels. Support models should be designed to be flexible, mapping to developer segmentation. Developers need access to sandbox environments, must be able to raise issues with support teams via a number of channels and must be able to rely on continuously updated and accurate documentation. Several of the companies that we work with have highlighted content as being the first line of support. Using artificial intelligence and automation allows a broader base of developers to be handled more quickly, efficiently and cost effectively while simultaneously enabling a state of continuous improvement.

While, according to our survey, developers want the right answer quickly, they rate knowledgeable support as more important than timely support by a small margin. Getting it right trumps getting it quickly if a trade-off is required. As with content, workhorses and experienced developers rate timely and knowledgeable support higher in importance than those who program less or are less experienced.

Marketing is a company's main channel for attracting developers and success is grounded in how well the platform segments and understands them. The needs of solo developers seeking support once per month are considerably different from those of an enterprise developer visiting daily or an executive at a large IT services company responsible for thousands of developers.

Market relevance ("has the platform stood the test of time and will it continue to do so?") is an important foundational element to developers, particularly professional developers. Nearly 90 percent rate market relevance as important compared to 64 percent of hobbyist developers. Thought leadership - or being first to market with points of view that embrace emerging technology - is considered by developers in China to be the most important aspect of developer ecosystem marketing.

Programs such as hackathons, developer days and conferences can help to attract and engage developers, provide the opportunity for face-to-face interaction and enable the creation of developer relationships and emotional connections with the platform. Activities such as webinars and tutorials, or establishing a learning & certification track can help to activate developers, allowing them to grow their expertise in your platform and augment their individual skill set.

The final consideration for me is Analytics, which enables product teams to keep their finger on the pulse of their developer community, provides a invaluable source of intelligence for product innovation and extracts effective insights from from the developer ecosystem. In addition to increased operational efficiencies, this can provide highly valuable inputs back to product engineering for feature development and roadmap integration. As an example demonstrating the benefits of harnessing analytics-enabled, data-driven insights, we have worked with a large internet company where the data analysis has highlighted the exact areas in which to engage with intelligent automation and process refinement. This has resulted in a 30% increase in the number of cases handled in one month, without the need to increase engineer headcount, an 12% increase in overall quality metrics and enabled the provision of developer-led field insights, 100+ of which have resulted in major product and developer experience improvements.

Developers consistently tell us via surveys that they value productivity above all else, and want documentation, sample code, development tools and tutorials plus answers on forums and technical support. It seems that you can

never over-produce on these, so how do you encourage the community to help you create/edit your technical content?
Community participation can be a hugely valuable asset. It can also be a challenge to set up, maintain and obtain value from. I have seen it be both successful and unsuccessful in areas as diverse as content moderation, support, bug-fixing, feature development and even event organization and management.

You need to start with some fundamentals. What is it that you would like the community to help you with? Examples could include flagging or editing a knowledge base, commenting on forum posts or providing answers, moderating or removing comments on your forum and testing for, and reporting, bugs. Having chosen the areas, you then need to think about the criticality of the function, the potential impact on your developer base, the resource commitment required, and the feasibility of this commitment being satisfied by the small percentage of your community who are willing to pitch in. Then you evaluate the critical mass within your developer community, how active they are, who the active members are (and have you consulted them?), what would incentivize them and what is the value exchange for them? Why are they interested in helping? Critical mass is a key consideration - for example, answers need to be provided within a short number of hours, if not minutes, if it's to be a resource that developers can rely on. If a question is asked without a timely response being given, then developers move on to another source and are unlikely to return.

There are a number of benefits to having your site form the community platform and supporting it yourself, such as immediacy of response, closer control over community activities and peace of mind in using your own infrastructure. This enables you to get information to your developer community instantly, which is highly valuable when launching a new product or service or communicating a critical bug fix or interim workaround. However, you can still encourage participation on the platform from the developer community. Allowing them to share their insights can generate a feeling of ownership, and a growing feeling of connection towards the platform, which helps to nurture community advocates. One area to consider closely however is risk - reputational, compliance, data, quality and security - and your comfort level with giving external developers access to some of the more secure areas of your infrastructure.

The second option, which for many companies may be considered more manageable, is to encourage growth of a solid community on a credible external site such as Stack Overflow. There is the benefit of getting the information from external sources, non-company affiliated (not Mom and Dad!), which can result in the answer carrying more weight. Third-party sites come with the critical mass of developers already in place, offer the ability to customize your presence on their site, enable arms-length moderation of the site by your own developers and wrap everything up in a solid analytics, insights and reporting package. Additionally, some developer groups, such as workhorse developers, are likely to prefer to be active on an aggregate site where they can build their reputation, interact with their peers and exhibit their knowledge, as opposed to engaging with a number of standalone forums or communities. Stack Overflow is a happy hunting ground for these guys. If workhorse developers are your target audience, then this may steer you away from investing in community moderation on your own platform.

A final thing to consider is how a community platform fits with the culture of your company, and with the culture of your developer base. This is important when evaluating the success and sustainability of harnessing your community. A good example here might be Mozilla, which epitomizes community, where the culture of the company fits extremely well with the community participation model with a large number of active volunteers and community participants.

What are some of the major issues you have seen with delivering technical content for developers, such as documentation?

If technical documentation is not created by a developer or someone with a technical background, it often seems to be written just to extol the virtues of the product, without telling developers what they need. They come to your site to read about your API and what it does, to learn how to build your code, or to download an SDK, or to get access to your API key. Or, they come when they get an error code or they encounter some specific problem and need to know what to do. If they find the documentation unhelpful, they go somewhere else, to a site like Stack Overflow. If your technical content is not written by the right people at the right level of detail, it will mean that your community of developers will go elsewhere.

While there's a case for developers writing guidance for other developers, there's a distinct skill, or a discipline, to technical writing. You need somebody that has a technical background, but with an understanding of product marketing and the ability to communicate the benefits of a product to the audience. There's an overlap needed between engineering skills, DevOps, product management, marketing and business awareness. The intersection is very small, and you need to find someone motivated to create documentation. Developers certainly aren't that keen on writing. In truth, you'll need to look beyond the engineering team and recruit people with the specific skills and enthusiasm for this kind of task. They can mentor and coach your developer team to make it self-sustainable over time.

Another problem with technical content is that it almost exclusively tends to be static. That means that almost as soon as it's written, it becomes obsolete. Companies tend to think of documentation as a one off, and that it doesn't evolve over time, so they can invest in it, or allocate budget for, it as a one off upfront cost. They don't see it as an ongoing investment. Dynamic content is what draws your developers back to the community and keeps them informed. It's why communities like Stack Overflow work so well. A small example here is where you have released a new build in one of your environments, and it's broken. You will get a notification from your community, and as soon as you get that you should have the ability or the facility to update your latest issues page or your knowledge base to highlight the issue. That first developer interaction enables all of the hundreds or thousands of developer interactions afterwards, and it should be as fluid and as interactive as possible.

Some staples of many developer programs (and big budget-eaters) like conferences, trade shows and meetups, hackathons and webinars appear near the bottom of developers' wish-lists in each survey we run. Yet many companies continue to offer them. Why? How can they increase their value?

It is true that grand events, such as a developer conference, can be a big budget-eater. It can also be difficult to quantify the somewhat intangible benefits. However, I feel that these activities deserve a place in your developer marketing strategy and whilst they may not be the optimal ways for developers to realize value from the product or service that the company offers, they do serve a purpose. In my experience they are often found far down the list of things that developers look for, but they tend to be well attended, can be effective in getting your message out there, are often vibrant in nature and can allow you to establish more of a 'real' connection with your developer community - potential developers can meet and interact with your actual developers.

The real value when evaluating such activities is to consider what your goals are, consider who you are trying to reach and what you are trying to achieve with that group. For example, are you trying to create awareness? Are you trying to increase adoption of your product or service? Are you trying to increase their skill and proficiency levels? Are you wanting to make them successful on your platform? Are you enabling developers to become advocates of your platform? The balance you are trying to achieve in these activities directly relates to the goals that you are trying to accomplish. If you can picture the developer engagement spectrum consisting of a number of stages, from Aware → Using → Proficient → Successful → Advocate then you will find that certain activities fit logically within specific stages. For example, a hackathon can be a great way to transition developers from "Aware" to "Using". You can determine which of these stage 'transitions' are of most value to you and to the developer groups that you are targeting and carry out a cost-benefit analysis that informs your investment strategy.

There may also be value to be found by looking in more detail at the developers who most derive value from your events and establishing why that is, simultaneously recognizing that the converse is also true. That exercise will necessitate a level of developer outreach activity, or harnessing whichever developer feedback mechanisms you have in place. Our research shows that traditional marketing - such as event frequency, variety, effectiveness, coolness and swag - is not valued as highly as other ecosystem elements but is still important to 65 percent of US developers. And it seems to be most important in countries that have a more nascent developer community than the US. For instance, 74 percent of China-based developers find frequent events to be important, which is a significantly higher percentage than in the US. As companies build out their developer ecosystem strategy globally, it is these sorts of important nuances that must be taken into consideration.

It is worth emphasizing the fact that distinct developer segments respond differently to conferences, trade shows and meetups, hackathons and webinars, and I have witnessed anecdotal evidence of this with some of the companies with which we work. For example, workhorse developers do not typically engage with platform companies on social media but are frequent attendees to digital events, especially ones that offer learning value. It feels like they are a number of critical components that need to be in place before considering the activities listed above. Gaining a deeper, more nuanced understanding of who is in the ecosystem is a good first step but an emphasis on improving content, education and support is also required. Rethinking the interactions and developer journeys can result in a more active and value-creating ecosystem.

Across the board there is ample opportunity to improve how companies promote their market position and communicate developer program capabilities. Only 20 percent of US developers strongly agree that developer ecosystems are generally good at marketing their capabilities to them. Improving effectiveness comes down to not just marketing, but understanding and serving the needs of the developers within your ecosystem.

We have a couple of great chapters about reaching out via content marketing over email marketing and social media. All the book's contributors are using these ways to communicate with developers to greater or lesser extent. Have you any best practices to share?

At a high level it all ties back to value and understanding the value proposition that the platform offers to developers. What problems do you help them to solve? You must know your audience and what they are most interested in and target your content specifically to them. You also need to consider how you get a direct handle on developer feedback, enabling you to learn and refine. Some of the companies that we work with have set up a developer feedback loop (internal and external) which helps them know what their developer community is thinking and feeling, helps them to stay ahead of emerging trends and allows them to continuously evolve.

Investing in understanding the developers who use your product, service, platform or software is paramount. This audience is key. If developers are unhappy, they will stop engaging, advocating and contributing: your product or service will struggle. In my experience, developers are a loyal bunch. They keep faith with companies that they respect and have a connection to; there is a store of trust in this symbiotic relationship that developers tap into and this can allow the platform a degree of leeway and forgiveness when things fail. However, this well of goodwill is not bottomless, and once it evaporates, it is extremely difficult to re-engage with those 'lost' developers. You need to always stay on top of the relationship, which requires significant investment in time and resources.

Another important practice is using a combination of channels, optimizing those that perform best for each segment of your developer base. Consider events, as an example that we previously discussed, in the context of your audience and your goals. Some people love events, and some people don't. This logic holds true for content. The point is to stay focused on your audience, to ascertain what works for them and to make sure to provide that. It also helps to focus on what developers do respond to, to track the success of campaigns and outreach programs which will enable data-driven insights to inform your future engagement strategy.

Platform companies that stand out among their competitors offer developers the chance to solve challenging problems in interesting ways. The most successful companies in this area:

- Inspire developers, by continually pushing technology boundaries and expanding the art of the possible.

- Trust developers, by open-sourcing code and granting access to libraries and repositories.

- Educate developers, by providing continually updated and comprehensive learning and certification programs.

- Inform developers, by providing relevant and up-to-date information written exactly as developers need it to be written.

- Empower developers, by granting them frictionless and barrier-free self-service access to platform services.

- Support developers, by being there when needed most, in the ways that each developer group needs them to be.

- Engage developers, by understanding what developers need to be successful and enabling mutually valuable relationships to grow.

- Respect developers, by recognizing the value they provide, the knowledge they possess and that their collective success is intertwined with their own.

In return, the developers they engage help to drive user acquisition and product usage that leads to the platform's revenue growth and rising market valuation.

Finally, where are we headed? And what are the biggest challenges facing developer marketing teams at present? Do you think we will see Developer Relations departments in companies become standard, in much the same way that IT departments are commonplace now but were unusual 20 years ago?

The global developer population keeps on growing and diversifying. The demand for developer skills intensifies and expands. The pace of technological change and the ever-increasing competitive landscape continue to make attracting and retaining developers extremely challenging. Traditional industry boundaries fall; as an example, we find ourselves today in a world where a global search giant, a technology hardware company, a household appliance company and multinational ridesharing platform companies are competing head-to-head with traditional car makers and electric vehicle manufacturers in the autonomous vehicle space. They are not only competing in unfamiliar competitive waters but are direct rivals for developer talent, for third party integration partners, for technology partners, for content partners, for software partners and are vying to become the platform or the operating system of choice for developers. As a developer, how do you choose?

We are already starting to see real growth in the numbers of Developer Relations departments in the Bay Area, and other technology hotspots globally. I believe that a number of the contributors to this book, along with myself, are on the verge of being referred to as veterans (!) which gives you an idea of how long Developer Relations has been around as a discipline. I have seen it evolve with the increasing presence of Developer

Advocate teams, Technical Writing teams and Developer Marketing teams. These changes can also frequently necessitate a level of organizational restructuring. Many of the 'born-digital' companies that I work with ensure that budgeting in particular (along with areas such as performance management, recruiting, social channels) falls under the Engineering organization. This helps to ensure that the way in which developers are attracted, engaged, targeted and retained all fall under the watch of those most familiar with their wants and needs - fellow developers. I have also noticed an upsurge in the number, and size of, specialist disciplines as the industry continues to mature.

Outside of the technology industry it is certainly less prevalent. Whilst it is still an area that is yet to catch on in more traditional industries such as finance, resources or utilities it is my view is that all companies now need to consider this space. Meeting the specific needs of this growing, increasingly diverse and highly nuanced area is increasingly becoming of paramount importance but it's tough to do given developers are typically high functioning, self-proclaimed over-achievers (typically multilingual, multi-OS and multi-platform). It requires a depth of knowledge and understanding that these more traditional companies typically do not have, and their pivot towards the 'new' will also squeeze the developer ecosystem space.

Effectively implementing a successful developer ecosystem gives the opportunity to expand outside of your traditional core businesses, to diversify and mitigate risk and to ensure your continued relevance. And from our experience, when effort is made to deliver value to developers, they will respond. In our survey, a full 70 percent of US developers agreed that a platform offering a truly differentiated and meaningful developer ecosystem would get a much larger part of their business.

Developers have now become one of the most important stakeholders that businesses need to nurture. The competitive advantage that companies could get a short number of years ago, by engaging effectively with this group, has now become a strategic necessity, as emerging technologies become the next battlegrounds. Incumbent leaders are at risk of being disrupted. Those platforms who are most aggressive about understanding the needs of this critical business constituency and building the services and programs developers require, can stand out from the crowd and attract and retain developers in an increasingly competitive fight for their mindshare, loyalty, user relevance and growth. Many former industry titans (the communications industry springs to mind instantly, followed by retail) that have struggled to gain traction with developers, now find themselves on the brink of existence, if not already extinct.

Companies that succeed with developers, cater to their nuanced needs and evolve as developers do, will be the companies that succeed, period. I feel that the reverse is also true: companies that fail in this space will be the companies that fail, period.